The Cross

AN ANTHOLOGY

THOMAS NELSON PUBLISHERS

Nashville

Library of Congress Cataloging-in-Publication Data is available.

Published in Nashville, Tennessee by Thomas Nelson, Inc.

Printed in the United States of America
1 2 3 4 5 — 07 06 05 04 03

Table of Contents

- I Love to Tell the Story, *Katherine Hankey*
- Onlookers, Luci Shaw
- Crucifixion, *Eva Gore-Booth*
- Near the Cross, *Unknown*
- Gethsemane, *Annette von Droste-Hulshoff*
- Lament of Our Lady Under the Cross, *Anonymous*

Preface

If you are a lover of good literature, from Longfellow to Lucado, then you will enjoy the pages that follow. Each chapter holds a treasure trove of meditative pieces for personal devotion during the Easter season. *Thomas Nelson Reference and Electronic Publishing* is proud to present our second book in Nelson's Anthology Series. *The Cross* will provide you and your family with a collection of the best classic and contemporary literature about the dramatic events leading up to the death of our Lord Jesus.

Within this collection, we have included both secular and Christian writers to provide you with multiple perspectives, understandings, and experiences that surround the events of the Crucifixion. For this reason, we have compiled poems, short stories, hymns, quotations, and more from authors in many different languages, cultures, and epochs. With all these different writings, there are variant spellings throughout the book. From Latin to Old English, we have included, in some cases, the original language of the piece in which it was written. Be aware that we may have purposely chosen to adhere to the spelling of that time and language. With these diverse selections, we hope that you will come to understand Christ's sacrifice with a renewed sense of awe and wonder as you identify with the writers of different times and cultures.

To highlight some of the unique authors and pieces, we have provided brief biographies and trivia that we think you will find fascinating. These side notes will offer a bit more depth and background to the writers and writings so that you might have a greater appreciation for their inclusion in this collection. We have also placed the chapters in chronological order according to their event as recorded in the Gospels. With this event order, you can develop your own personal devotion during the Easter season.

Commemorate the dramatic events surrounding the Crucifixion, as seen through the eyes of the Gospels. From the tender assistance of Simon of Cyrene as he helped Jesus carry the burden of His cross, to the amazing confession of the Centurion who proclaimed, "Truly this is the Son of God!" Follow the path to Golgotha, witness the mocking and the death of Jesus, and feel the devotion of the women who wouldn't leave His side.

Now, turn the pages and experience the joy and sorrows of these writers as they delineate both the rejoicing and the suffering that surround the poignant story of our Savior's death.

"The Cross alone is our theology."
—MARTIN LUTHER

CHAPTER ONE

Simon of Cyrene

CHAPTER · ONE

Simon of Cyrene

LUKE 23:26
²⁶*Now as they led Him away, they laid hold of a certain man, Simon a Cyrenian, who was coming from the country, and on him* they laid the cross that he might bear it after Jesus.

Simon of Cyrene
(A Poetic Meditation by Simon of Cyrene)

Long and tedious was the road
that brought me to Jerusalem!
   How I longed
   for Passover!

Merchant shipping was delayed—
all conspired to make me late,
   almost late
   for Passover!

Late along the road I came,
saw the Temple glow like flame!
   How I longed
   for Passover!

Tiring, so I could not run,
trudging wearily must come,
   almost late
   for Passover!

Now I see a dusty cloud
swirling round a noisy crowd
 on the road
  to Calvary!

Passover I've come to eat,
not to see these marching feet
 on the road
  to Calvary!

Now I see one bruised and goaded,
stumbling under cross-bar loaded,
 on the road
  to Calvary!

Hand upon me, voice commanding,
"Take the cross and bear it for him!"
 on the road
  to Calvary!

Cross I carry, load I lighten,
yet my load he carries for me
 on that cross
  on Calvary!

Heavy beam that low had bowed him
bears him as my sin assails him
 on that cross
  on Calvary!

"It is finished!" hear him crying
as for me I see him dying
 on that cross
  on Calvary!

Passover—the lamb is slain,
bearing all my guilt and pain
on that cross
on Calvary!
—Peter J. Blackburn
From *Between the Lines:*
Dialogues for Worship

This meditation represents reminiscences of Simon at a much later time when he has reflected on the events of that day in the light of Christian faith. And the name and experience of Simon would surely not have appeared in the gospel record if he had not become a member of the Christian community.

Simon of Cyrene—Cross Bearer

As Jesus was carrying his cross out of Jerusalem to the place of execution, a man named Simon of Cyrene was coming in (Mt. 27:32; P 15:21; L 23:26), and the soldiers compelled him to carry the cross of Jesus. (The word Angareuo (Greek Gamma Gamma corresponds to English ng as in "finger"), here used for "compel," is a technical one, perhaps better translated "impress," and referring to the legal right of a soldier to require a provincial to carry his gear one mile for him. The word occurs in the New Testament only here and in Matthew 5:41.)

Mark calls him "the father of Alexander and Rufus" without further explanation, apparently taking it for granted that his readers would all know who Rufus and Alexander are. The Christian writer Papias (who died around 130) tells us that Mark originally wrote his Gospel for the Christian community in Rome. This suggests that Alexander and Rufus were well known to, and probably part of, the Christian congregation in Rome. Very possibly their father Simon had himself become a Christian, though this must remain conjecture.

—James E. Kiefer
From *The Society of Archbishop Justus* website

The Prince of the House of David
(*Excerpt*)

"But he [Jesus] had no strength to advance three steps with it, though he made the effort to obey his tyrannous executioners. At this crisis they discerned a Syro-Phoenician merchant, Simon of Cyrene, a venerable man, well-known to all in Jerusalem, and father of the two young men, Rufus and Alexander, who were followers of Jesus, having sold, the last year, all they had, in order to become his disciples, and sit at his feet, and listen to his Divine teachings. Their father was, for this, or some other reason, particularly obnoxious to Caiaphas, and, on seeing him, he pointed him out to the Centurion, "as one of the Nazarene," and suggested that he should be compelled to bear the cross after him.

The Cyrenian merchant was at once dragged from his mule, and led to the place where the cross lay, believing he was about to be himself executed. But when he beheld Jesus standing, pale and bleeding, by the fallen cross, and knew what was required of him, he burst into tears, and kneeling at his feet, said:

"If they compel me to do this, Lord, think not that I aid thy death! I know that thou art a Prophet come from God! If thou diest today, Jerusalem will have more precious blood to answer for than the blood of all her prophets."

"We brought thee here not to prate, old man, but to work. Thou art strong-bodied. Up with this end of the cross, and go on after him!" cried the chief priests.

Simon, who is a powerful man, though three-score years of age, raised the extremity of the beam, and Jesus essayed to move under the weight of the other; but he failed.

"Let me bear it alone, Master," answered the stout Simon, "I am the stronger. Thou hast enough to bear the weight of thine own sorrow. If it be a shame to bear a cross after thee, I glory in my shame, as would my two sons, were they here this day."

Thus speaking in a courageous and bold voice, and looking as brace as if he would as gladly be nailed to the cross for his Master, as carry it after him (for Simon had long believed in him, as well as his sons), he lifted the cross upon his shoulders, and ascended the steep after Jesus, who, weak from loss of blood and of sleep, and weary unto death, had to lean, for support, against one arm of the instrument of death.

> *"Let me bear it alone, Master." said Simon. "I am the stronger."*

Ah, my dear father, what a place was this, up which we climbed! Skulls lay scattered beneath our footsteps, and everywhere human bones bleached in the air; and we trode in heaps of ashes, where the Romans had burned the bodies of those whom they crucified.

At length we reached the top of this hill of death, on which five crosses were already standing. Upon one of them a criminal still hung, just alive, who had been nailed to it the noon before. He called feebly for water, but some derided, and all passed him unheeded. There was an empty space on the summit, and here the Centurion stopped, and ordered the crosses to be set in the rock, where deep holes had been already cut for them. The crosses carried by the thieves were now thrown down by them; by one with an execration, by the other with a sigh, as he anticipated the anguish he was to suffer upon it.

The larger cross of the three was that for Jesus. It was taken by three soldiers from the back of the old Cyrenian merchant, and thrown heavily upon the earth. It was now that a crisis approached, of the most painful interest. The Centurion ordered his soldiers to clear a circle about the place, where the crosses were to be planted, with their spears. The Jews, who had crowded near, in eager thirst for their victim's blood, gave back slowly and reluctantly, before the sharp points of the Roman lances, pushed against their breasts; for the Centurion had with him full three-score men-at-arms, besides a part of Herod's guard. So great was the desire of the Jews to get near, that helpless females could not be otherwise than crowded away from the immediate scene."

—J. H. INGRAHAM
From *The Prince of the House of David*

What My Obedience to God Costs Other People

"They laid hold upon one Simon . . . and on him they laid the cross."
—LUKE 23:26

If we obey God it is going to cost other people more than it costs us, and that is where the sting comes in. If we are in love with our Lord, obedience does not cost us anything, it is a delight, but it costs those who do not love Him a good deal. If we obey God it will mean that other people's plans are upset, and they will gibe us with it—"You call this Christianity?" We can prevent the suffering; but if we are going to obey God, we must not prevent it, we must let the cost be paid.

Our human pride entrenches itself on this point, and we say—I will never accept anything from anyone. We shall have to, or disobey God. We have no right to expect to be in any other relation than our Lord Himself was in.

Stagnation in spiritual life comes when we say we will bear the whole thing ourselves. We cannot. We are so involved in the universal purposes of God that immediately when we obey God, others are affected. Are we going to remain loyal in our obedience to God and go through the humiliation of refusing to be independent, or are we going to take the other line and say— I will not cost other people suffering? We can disobey God if we choose, and it will bring immediate relief to the situation, but we shall be a grief to our Lord. Whereas if we obey God, He will look after those who have been pressed into the consequences of our obedience. We have simply to obey and to leave all consequences to Him.

> *We can prevent the suffering; but if we are going to obey God, we must let the cost be paid.*

Beware of the inclination to dictate to God as to what you will allow to happen if you obey Him.

—OSWALD CHAMBERS
From *My Utmost for His Highest*

OSWALD CHAMBERS (1874–1917)—Oswald Chambers' most famous devotional book, *My Utmost for His Highest,* began in 1908 when young Oswald, fresh from seminary, boarded a ship to America. He was assigned to escort a young woman named Gertrude Hobbs on that trip. They eventually married and began a ministry of Bible correspondence classes. During World War I, the Chambers began a ministry to troops in Egypt, but in 1917 Oswald died from complications after having his appendix removed. Mrs. Chambers returned home and began transcribing all of her notes from his lectures. In 1923, *My Utmost for His Highest* was published and to this day, continues to encourage and challenge thousands of readers.

Men Follow Simon

They spat in his face and hewed him a cross
On that dark day.
The cross was heavy; Simon bore it
Golgotha way.
   O Master, the cross is heavy!

They ripped his hands with driven nails
And flayed him with whips.
They pressed the sponge of vinegar
To his parched lips.
   O Master, thy dear blood drips!

Men follow Simon, three and three,
And one and one,
Down through valleys and up long hills
Into the sun.
   O Master, Master—into the sun!

          —RAYMOND KRESENSKY
        From *Christ in Poetry of Today*

Prayer

Traditional Language

Heavenly Father, whose most dear Son, as He walked the way of the Cross, accepted the service of Simon of Cyrene to carry his physical burden for him: mercifully grant unto each of us the grace that we may gladly bear one another's burdens, for the love of him who said, "Inasmuch as ye have done it unto the least of these my brethren, ye have done it unto me," even the same thy Son Jesus Christ our Lord, who now liveth and reigneth with thee and the Holy Ghost, one God, now and for ever.

> *Jesus accepted the service of Simon of Cyrene to carry his physical burden for Him.*

Contemporary Language

Heavenly Father, whose most dear Son, as He walked the way of The Cross, accepted the service of Simon of Cyrene to carry his physical burden for him: grant us each the grace gladly to bear one another's burdens, for the love of him who said, "As you did it to the least of these my brethren, you did it to me," your Son Jesus Christ our Lord, who now lives and reigns with you and the Holy Spirit, one God, now and for ever.

—JAMES E. KIEFER
From *The Society of Archbishop Justus* website

The Cross of Christ

"Like Simon of Cyrene we carry the cross, for he calls us to take it up and follow him."

—JOHN STOTT
From *The Cross of Christ*

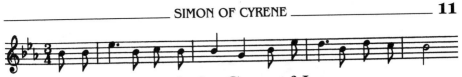

Beneath the Cross of Jesus

Beneath the cross of Jesus I fain would take my stand,
The shadow of a mighty rock within a weary land;
A home within the wilderness, a rest upon the way,
From the burning of the noontide heat, and the burden of the day.
O safe and happy shelter, O refuge tried and sweet,
O trysting place where Heaven's love and Heaven's justice meet!
As to the holy patriarch that wondrous dream was given,
So seems my Savior's cross to me, a ladder up to heaven.
There lies beneath its shadow but on the further side
The darkness of an awful grave that gapes both deep and wide
And there between us stands the cross two arms outstretched to save
A watchman set to guard the way from that eternal grave.
Upon that cross of Jesus mine eye at times can see
The very dying form of One Who suffered there for me;
And from my stricken heart with tears two wonders I confess;
The wonders of redeeming love and my unworthiness.
I take, O cross, thy shadow for my abiding place;
I ask no other sunshine than the sunshine of His face;
Content to let the world go by to know no gain or loss,
My sinful self my only shame, my glory all the cross.

—ELIZABETH C. CLEPHANE
From *Family Treasury*

ELIZABETH C. CLEPHANE (1830–1869)—Although physically frail, Elizabeth Clephane was known for her helpful, cheery nature. She grew up in Melrose, Scotland where she served the poor and sick of her community and donated to charity anything left after meeting her own minimal needs. Elizabeth, who was known to the townspeople as "the sunbeam," enjoyed writing and was consistently published in the Scottish Presbyterian magazine, *The Family Treasury*. However, the majority of her writings appeared anonymously. Elizabeth died at the tender age of 39.

Remember Jesus Christ
(Excerpt)

There was Simon of Cyrene, described as one "coming out of the country"; him the soldiers seized and compelled to carry the cross of Christ to the place of execution. He might be regarded as the first in that great multitude who have followed Christ, each bearing a cross. On the other hand, the role of Simon was absolutely unique. None other can share the weight of that redeeming, atoning cross, and no one is compelled to follow Christ. Burdens are laid upon us, but only in free will can one "take up his cross."

—CHARLES R. ERDMAN

Voices from Calvary
(Excerpt)

Exhausted by the events of the night, and the sufferings of His body, with His strength sapped by lack of refreshment and by spiritual anguish such as man never knew, Jesus was unable to bear the weight of His own cross, and so they cast about for a substitute. What an amazing thought that is! He Who came from heaven's courts to be the sinner's substitute, in His hour of physical need required one for Himself!

As the soldiers cast their eyes over the assembled crowd, their gaze fell upon a tall man from Africa. This man must have towered about the mob, so as to be easily distinguished. He was a powerful man, able to bear the weight of the cross. It must not be thought for a second that Simon was a willing substitute. Indeed, the contrary was the case. It must be remembered that Simon was not a Negro; he was a Jew who traced his ancestry back to a high and proud descent from Abraham. Cyrene was a Jewish colony on the coast of Africa, and from there this African of Jewish blood had journeyed to the Holy City.

According to the law of Moses, Simon was a godly man. He was in the city of Jerusalem for the feast of the Passover. It is highly probable that this was the first time that privilege ever had been his. He would not have been called "the Cyrene" if it were not that he had been born, or at least raised, in that distant colony. The heart of every true son of Israel turned to the city of Jerusalem for the Passover season, to celebrate that sacred feast in the city that was peculiarly the place of God. That was the aspiration and dream of every Jew who lived beyond the confines of Palestine. Simon knew the law of Moses, and he undoubtedly realized that if he touched an instrument of execution, he became ceremonially unclean.

So aside from the natural abhorrence, with which any normal man greets the gallows, Simon was faced with the tragic certainty that if he so much as touched the cross, it would frustrate the purpose of this Passover. Perhaps, also, for years he had saved out of a meager income, that he might have the means to celebrate this sacred feast in the city of Jerusalem. And now on the threshold of the house of his desire, he is suddenly laid hold of by the soldiers of Rome, and compelled to bear this cross.

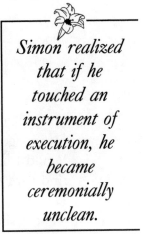

Simon realized that if he touched an instrument of execution, he became ceremonially unclean.

In a word, Simon was drafted! All the versions of the gospel that contain this striking and dramatic episode say, "Him they compelled to bear the cross." His very soul seethed with hate as he perforce complied with the soldiers' demand. What a contrast between the two who laid hold on that cross! Simon, who bore it in bitterness and anguish of spirit, his heart's blood almost curdled with hatred; and Jesus, Who bore it in love! His whole being was imbued with the glory of the sacrifice that He made because of God's love for a sinful world!

The hatred of Simon was, of course, primarily directed at Rome. All of the bitterness and anger natural in the Jewish heart toward the political oppressor of his people now becomes personal and personified, as Rome robs him of the sacred joy of participating in the Passover feast.

In his heart as well there must have been hatred for Jesus, Who was the innocent cause of Simon's frustration.

But this man who turned away from God's temple unfitted to enter, lived to boast in later years with streaming eyes of his deed on that day! Our hearts rejoice to note in later history how Simon became a power in the church. His sons are named in the church of the apostolic age where they were deacons. The mighty Paul sends greeting to one of Simon's sons in the Roman Epistle, where the wife of Simon is also saluted by the great apostle. There was no gathering of the saints of Christ in that first century that did not feel honored when Simon entered. His coming hallowed every service, and his very presence was a benediction. We can see this tall, sun-browned man of Africa standing in that company of the early saints and humbly but joyfully telling how he helped Jesus Christ redeem the world from the grasp of Satan, and open heaven's door to the lost.

—HARRY RIMMER

The Crosse

Since Christ embraced the Crosse itself, dare I,
His image, the image of his Crosse deny?
Would I have profit by the sacrifice,
And dare the chosen altar to despise?
It bore all other sins, but is it fit
That it should bear the sin of scorning it?

—JOHN DONNE

JOHN DONNE (1572–1631)—After attending the prestigious universities of Oxford and Cambridge, John Donne refused degrees from both places on religious grounds. He had been raised Catholic. He went on to study law and receive a position as a secretary for a statesman. While pursuing this career, he was imprisoned for marrying the young Anne More without her parents' consent. After being released, he and Anne lived in poverty due to his inability to obtain work. While writing poetry, he succumbed to his peers and became an ordained minister of the Church of England, renouncing his ties to Catholicism. A mere two years later, his beloved Anne died. Obsessed with death, John began to write his best metaphysical poetry and continued writing until his death in 1631.

The Gospel According to Luke:
Exposition & Application
(Excerpt)

Roman custom required the condemned to carry his own cross to the place of execution. This, apparently, Jesus was unable to do, thanks to the scourging he had undergone. Scourging was a most cruel punishment under which the victim sometimes died; the thongs, weighted with sharp metal or bone, drew blood at every blow. So a bystander, one Simon of Cyrene, was ordered to relieve him.

We should like to know more about Simon. The circumstance that he came from a town in North Africa gave rise to the belief (most probably unwarranted) that he was Negro. Hence Countee Cullen's poem entitled "Simon the Cyrenian Speaks":

> *He never spoke a word to me,*
> *And yet He called my name;*
> *He never gave a sign to me,*
> *And yet I knew and came.*
>
> *At first I said, "I will not bear*
> *His cross upon my back;*
> *He only seeks to place it there*
> *Because my skin is black."*
>
> *But He was dying for a dream,*
> *And He was very meek,*
> *And in His eyes there shone a gleam*
> *Men journey far to seek.*
>
> *It was Himself my pity bought;*
> *I did for Christ alone*
> *What all of Rome could not have wrought*
> *With bruise of lash or stone.*

16

The one thing we know for certain about Simon (in addition to his place of residence) is that he was the father of Alexander and Rufus, who, apparently, were well known in the early Church (Mark 15:21).

> *Roman custom required the condemned to carry his own cross to the place of execution.*

This perhaps tells us much. Was Simon's strange encounter with Jesus a crisis and turning point in his own life? Did the divineness of Jesus' character as revealed in his closing hours lead Simon to become an inquirer and presently a disciple? Did he return to his home in North Africa a professed Christian, and bring up his sons in the Christian faith, and have the satisfaction of seeing them take an active part in the Christian movement? This conjecture is attractive, and is moreover, in line with Christian experience—"We know that in everything God works with those who love him, whom he has called in accordance with his purpose, to bring about what is good" (Romans 8:28 Goodspeed). It is conceivable that in this case God worked through the necessity for someone to carry the cross on which his "own Son" (Romans 8:32) was condemned to die.

—ERNEST FREMONT TITTLE

St. Simon of Cyrene
(For the Spirit of James Wright)

When I edged over to gape and gawk, I caught
The soldiers lifting up a man.
Grabbing me by the scruff, I fought
The weight, the splinters, and their pagan hands,
How the women wept on the spattered stone
And beat their breasts; how from the angry fray
Their voices rose as He lay prone
While I shouldered His pain along the way.

Bruised for life, I found his friends in retreat,
Scared, broken, and wondering why? Trying to cope
Inside, I went to their secret place:
Then I remembered wood that tripped his feet,
The hands that fixed him to the wood. When he spoke,
Something of love lightly caressed my face.

—RICHARD S. WILSON
From The Franciscan Friars Third
Order website

They Met at Calvary
(Excerpt)

I know he was compelled to do it. A prisoner was supposed to carry his own cross to the place of execution, but our blessed Lord could not do it. Weakened by the bloody sweat, and the lashings of the pillar, and all the burden of the world's pain thrust through the channels of his mighty heart, he fell beneath the load.

The soldiers caught hold of a man in the crowd and made him carry the cross. I don't suppose he wanted to. I imagine he felt as you would feel, if you were looking on at some trouble in the streets and were suddenly pounced upon to take part in it. Your first thought would be: "I want to keep out of this." But when he was dragged forward and saw that piteous, bloodstained figure, and the unearthly look of the Son of God, don't you think some pity stirred in his heart? Don't you think he said within himself: "Well, I am not going to be crucified, but I can at least carry the cross for him"? Anyhow, he did. He carried the cross for Jesus. I am grateful to Simon of Cyrene for that."

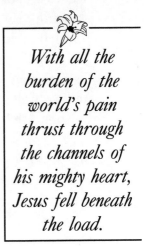

With all the burden of the world's pain thrust through the channels of his mighty heart, Jesus fell beneath the load.

—W. E. SANGSTER

Simon the Cyrene

I was on my way to the fields when I saw Him
   carrying His cross;
  and multitudes were following Him.
  Then I too walked beside Him.
His burden stopped Him many a time, for His body
   was exhausted.
Then a Roman soldier approached me, saying,
  "Come, you are strong and firm built;
  carry the cross of this man."
When I heard these words my heart swelled within me
   and I was grateful.
  And I carried His cross.
It was heavy, for it was made of poplar
   soaked through with the rains of winter.
And Jesus looked at me. And the sweat of His forehead
   was running down upon His beard.
Again He looked at me and He said, "Do you too
   drink this cup?
You shall indeed sip its rim with me to the end of
   time."
So saying He placed His hand upon my free shoulder.
And we walked together towards the Hill of the Skull.
But now I felt not the weight of the cross.
  I felt only His hand.
And it was like the wing of a bird upon my shoulder.
Then we reached the hill top,
  and there they were to crucify Him.
  And then I felt the weight of the tree.
He uttered no word when they drove the nails
   into His hands and feet, nor made He any sound.
And His limbs did not quiver under the hammer.

It seemed as if He sought the nails
   as the prince would seek the sceptre;
   and that He craved to be raised to the heights.
And my heart did not think to pity Him,
   for I was too filled with wonder.
Now, the man whose cross I carried has become my
   cross.
Should they say to me again, "Carry the cross of this
   man,"
I would carry it till my road ended at the grave.
But I would beg Him to place His hand upon my
   shoulder.
This happened many years ago;
   and still whenever I follow the furrow in the field,
   and in that drowsy moment before sleep,
I think always of that Beloved Man.
And I feel His winged hand, here, on my left shoulder.

                             —KAHLIL GIBRAN

Assistants at the Passion
(Excerpt)

The sentiment of the Church canonized the centurion who presided over the crucifixion of Jesus. It also canonized the penitent robber who appears in the calendar as St. Bonus Latro. But although there is a tradition that he afterwards became a Christian, the Church has not canonized Simon of Cyrene.

He was a conspicuous figure in the thought of the Apostolic Church. He is mentioned by name in the first three Gospels; his sons, Alexander and Rufus, are spoken of as though they were well-known Christians; but the Church, so far as I know, has given to Simon no mark of her approbation.

I take him, then, as the man who is forced by cruel necessity to carry the cross of Jesus, whose will consents to the extent of animating his body to do the material task, and no further. The suggestion of the story is that he was a well-known settler from Cyrene in North Africa, that he lived on the outskirts of the city and was coming into town in the ordinary way in the morning, having heard nothing of the disturbance of the previous night. By what he would regard as an appalling stroke of misfortune, he was passing through the city gate just as the death procession was coming out, and at the moment when our Lord's strength collapsed under the weight of the cross. The scourging had made it physically impossible for the condemned to carry the wood of His cross all the way. There was a moment of difficulty; no one in the crowd would touch the defiling boards, and the soldiers in a flash of inspiration caught and impressed this strong, solid, comfortable-looking man into their service, and thrust the blood-stained boards upon him. There was nothing for it but to set his teeth, square his shoulders, and do the job. It must have taken him some time to recover from the shock of the incident, and while he was doing his best to forget it, it would have seemed the delusion of a madman to think that, forget it as he might, it would cause him to be held in eternal remembrance. "If any man will come after Me, let him deny himself, and take up his cross and follow Me."

> *Every man who does not of his own free will accept the Cross is caught and forced to carry it against his will.*

My point is this: every single man who does not of his own free will accept the Cross is caught and forced to carry it against his will. There is no escaping the Cross altogether. Everyone must carry the Cross willingly or unwillingly.

For consider! We are all the product of a civilization that is based on Christian ethics and many centuries of it have produced an almost intolerably sensitive race of people. These are the people on whom the curse of the Cross is resting, the people who refuse to accept the principle upon which their civilization is based, but who cannot escape from the situation it has created. These are the followers of Simon of Cyrene.

It is a profoundly pathetic fact that all the best of our unwilling cross-bearers have an ideal of conduct in the matter. To the good-hearted man who has never accepted the principle of the Cross, the highest conduct consists in taking it up and carrying it under the impetus of a sort of moral necessity.

He will always match your story of a Saint with a story of a man who was anything but a Saint, but who, nevertheless, did the same thing. And he will always suggest to you that his man did a finer thing in doing the noble action from an unexplained involuntary impulse than your saint who was moved to the same action by Christian principle. In other words, supposing Simon of Cyrene, when he saw what he was expected to do, did it con amore, and offered our Lord, moved by an impulse of compassion, a ready and sympathetic assistance, the unwilling cross-bearer would consider him one of the noblest characters in the Gospels, and would be extremely contemptuous of the judgment of the Church, who has canonized the man who said, "Lord, remember me when Thou comest into Thy Kingdom," but has not canonized the good-hearted fellow who did what the unwilling cross-bearer calls "such an awfully decent thing."

—Rev. H. F. B. Mackay

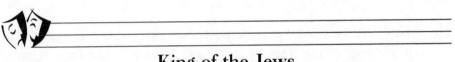

King of the Jews
(A Play)

Hushim—*A woman of the tribe of Benjamin; wife of Simon and mother of his two sons, Alexander and Rufus;* Simon—*Of Cyrene, who owns a field in the country outside Jerusalem, on the way to Bethel.*

The Scene: Jerusalem

Time: The First Hour on the day of Preparation.

Hushim: Now you know what to do, don't you? You go to the Temple by the second hour and wait for Joad. You'll know Joad, he'll be dressed as a priest. Tell Joad he's the handsomest man you've ever seen; he's small, you know, and likes to think he's captivating. Compliment the High Priest on his sense of justice; say it is the finest in the world; anything . . . . Don't be afraid of overdoing it; all men love flattery.

SIMON: [*nods his head*] I'll do my best.

HUSHIM: If I've not heard from you by the fourth hour I'll send Alexander to you to know the result, for I shall be very anxious. And the boy'll find out, he's so sharp. Don't spare compliments. You must be doorkeeper in the Temple, and flattery is like honey, even if you don't deserve it, it's pleasant.

SIMON: [*going*] I'll try to do what you say, Hushim.

The Eleventh Hour on the day of Preparation.

HUSHIM: Well? Have you got the post? You have been a time. Are you a doorkeeper of the Temple; have we a house in the Inner Court?

SIMON: [*passing his hand over his forehead*] I don't know.

HUSHIM: Don't know; you must know. Was Joad there? He promised to speak for you. Did you see him?

SIMON: I didn't see him. [*Sits down wearily.*]

HUSHIM: Didn't see him? Wasn't he there? My uncle's brother, too, and he promised me: The liar. What did you do?

SIMON: I did nothing. I'm tired, Hushim.

HUSHIM: Tired! What happened? Why don't you speak? What's the matter with you? Are you dumb or ill?

SIMON: I'm not ill, I'm only tired.

HUSHIM: Tired, you great hulk. Where have you been? What have you been doing? What's the matter with you? Can't you speak?

SIMON: If you knew—

HUSHIM: If I knew what? Oh, you make me mad. What is it? [*She takes him by the shoulder and shakes him.*] What's happened? Oh, you brute.

SIMON: You've no cause for anger, wife.

HUSHIM: No Cause! Have you got the place? What did the High Priest say? You must know that.

SIMON: I don't know.

HUSHIM: You don't know. You must be mad. This comes of marrying a foreigner, a fool, a great brute. They all said I'd repent. Oh! Oh! Oh!

SIMON: Don't cry, Hushim. I'll tell you everything.

HUSHIM: [*drying her eyes*] Tell me, did they make you doorkeeper? That's what I want to know. Tell me that. You promised you'd be in the Temple at the second hour, and here it is the eleventh. Where have you been all day? Where?

SIMON: I'm sorry, wife; I forgot.

HUSHIM: Forgot, sorry! What do you mean? Joad promised me to get you the place if the High Priest liked you. Did you get it? What did they say? Talk, man.

SIMON: I'm so sorry. I forgot all about it. I have not been to the Temple.

HUSHIM: You've not been to the Temple, and why not? Where were you? Don't say that Eli got the post. Don't say it or I'll strike you.

SIMON: I'm very sorry. I forgot. I don't know who got it. I wasn't there.

HUSHIM: [*sitting down*] Oh! OH! Oh! He wasn't there! OH! Oh! Oh! Where have you been all these hours? What have you been doing? Where did you go? Where did you eat?

SIMON: I've not eaten. I've—

HUSHIM: Not eaten! Why not? What's happened? Oh, why won't you speak? Talk, tell me!

SIMON: I'll tell you everything; but I'm very tired.

HUSHIM: Tell me first, who got the post? You must have heard.

SIMON: I don't know. I've not heard.

HUSHIM: At the fourth hour I sent Alexander to the Temple to find out whether you were chosen or not; when it got so dark I sent Rufus to my sister-in-law, Hoshed. I could not bear the suspense. They've both come back without news. You must know who got the post.

SIMON: No, I don't know. I didn't ask, but—

HUSHIM: You didn't ask?

SIMON: I'm thirsty.

HUSHIM: [*giving him wine*] There! Now tell me everything. You went out to the field?

SIMON: [*nods while drinking the wine*] I was at the field till nearly the second hour working, then I came into the city. When I reached the street which leads from the Temple to Golgotha I could not get across it, there was such a crowd. They had all come to see some prisoners who were going to be crucified.

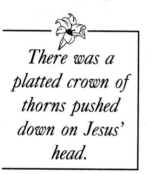

There was a platted crown of thorns pushed down on Jesus' head.

HUSHIM: But didn't you push through?

SIMON: I got through to the first file, but there soldiers kept the passage. I had to wait. No one was allowed to cross . . . They told me there were three criminals. The people were talking about them. Two were thieves and one was a rebel from the north, who had tried to make himself king. It was to see him the people had run together. Some said he was a Holy Man . . .

After a little while the prisoners came by. The two thieves first, and then slowly the man, whom some called prophet. He looked very ill . . . [*After a long pause.*] They had platted a crown of thorns and pushed it down on his head, and the thorns had torn the flesh and the blood ran down his face. When he came opposite to me he fell and lay like a dead man; the Cross was heavy . . . The Centurion ordered some of the Roman soldiers to lift the cross from him and he got up. He seemed very weak and frail: he could hardly stand . . . The Centurion came across to me and pulled me out, and pointed to the Cross and told me to shoulder it and get on . . .

HUSHIM: But why you?

SIMON: I suppose because I looked big and strong.

HUSHIM: Didn't you tell him you had to be at the Temple?

SIMON: Of course I told him, but he thrust me forward and warned me if I didn't do as I was told I'd have to go to the Temple without feet.

HUSHIM: Oh, what bad luck! No one ever had such bad luck as you. No one. Why didn't you run away?

SIMON: I didn't think—

HUSHIM: Well, you carried the Cross? And then—

SIMON: I went to lift the Cross; it seemed as if I were helping to punish the man. While I stood hesitating, he looked at me, Hushim. I never saw such eyes or such a look. Somehow or other I knew he wanted me to do it. I lifted the Cross up and got my shoulder under it and walked on. I did not seem to notice the weight of it, I was thinking of his look, and so we went through the crowd past Golgotha to the Hill of Calvary. On the top I put down the Cross.

HUSHIM: When was that? It must have been about the third hour. Why didn't you go to the Temple then? You see, it was all your fault. I knew it was! But go on, go on.

SIMON: I forgot all about the Temple. I could think of nothing but the Holy Man. He stood there so quiet while the priests and people jeered at him . . . . When they nailed the others up they shrieked and screamed and cursed. It was dreadful . . . When they were getting ready to nail him to the Cross I went over to him and said, "O Master," and he turned to me, "forgive me, Master, for doing what your enemies wished." And he looked at me again, and my heart turned to water, and the tears streamed from my eyes, I don't know why . . . He put his hands on my shoulder and said, "Friend, friend, there is nothing to forgive . . ." [*Lays his head on his arms and sobs.*]

HUSHIM: Don't cry, Simon, don't cry. He must have been a prophet!

SIMON: [*choking*] If you had seen him. If you had seen his eyes . . .

HUSHIM: [*beginning to cry*] I know, I know. What else did he say?

SIMON: He thanked me, and though I was a foreigner and a stranger to him, and quite rough and common, he took me in his arms and kissed me. I was all broken before him . . . He was wonderful. When they nailed him to the Cross he did not even groan—not a sound. And when they lifted the Cross up—the worst torture of all—he just grew white, white . . . All the priests and the people mocked him and asked him if he could save others why he couldn't save himself. But he answered not a word . . .

> *Above His head on the Cross, they had written, "King of the Jews."*

I could have killed them, the brutes! He prayed to God to forgive them, and he comforted one of the thieves who was sobbing in pain . . . Oh, he was wonderful. Even in his anguish he could think of others, and yet he was the weakest of all . . .

And then the storm burst, and I stood there for hours and hours in the darkness. I could not leave him, I wanted . . . Later some of his own people came about the Cross, weeping, his mother and his followers, and took him down, and they called him Master and Lord, as I had called him. They had all loved him. They all loved him. No one could help loving him, no one . . .

Above his head on the Cross, they had written, "King of the Jews." You Jews have no king, I know; they did it to mock him. But he was a King, king of the hearts of men.

HUSHIM: And with all that, we've lost the place! What was his name?

SIMON: Jesus of Nazareth.

HUSHIM: What was it he said to you? I want to remember to tell Hoshed.

SIMON: He called me "Blessed, for that I, a stranger, who did not even know him, was the only man in the world who had ever helped to bear his burden."

—FRANK HARRIS
From *The Passion Drama*

The Day of the Cross
(Excerpt)

In the early history of Israel it would have been impossible to find a Hebrew beyond the shadow of the rugged mountain ridge that lifts itself between the Jordan and the Mediterranean Sea. With a stubborn loyalty, born of the memory of a great spiritual past, and nourished by the hopes of a greater future, the Hebrews clung to the hills which had been the sanctuary of their faith. But captivity and exile had bewildered the people's mind, long centuries of oppression and exaction had impoverished their land, and the later years of alien rule had broken their spirit. The Hebrew was weaned from his inborn love for his native soil, every high road that led out of Palestine saw the poverty stricken Jew leaving his desecrated land, and every city saw his unchanging features in its streets, and found his tireless energy competing in its industries.

But the Jew made no home in any of the countries in which the race was scattered abroad. Whether he went East or West, one spot held him in a holy devotion. Like the exiled Scot, who in his dreams beholds the Hebrides, the blue hills of Judea never sank below the horizon of the Hebrew imagination. "If I forget thee, O Jerusalem, let my right hand forget her cunning," was the psalm that stirred his heart. And in these families of the twelve tribes scattered abroad, sons were born, who were given the great names of Moses and Samuel, and Jacob, and Simeon, and Saul, and Benjamin, and taught to read, with an enthralling patriotism, the story of Abraham's faith, and to chant the psalms of Israel. And then

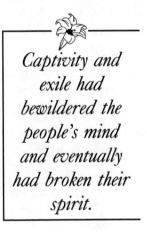

Captivity and exile had bewildered the people's mind and eventually had broken their spirit.

they grew to manhood, the fire dwindled by their fathers devotion burst into a flame of desire to see Jerusalem, to walk the streets of the city where God had chosen to make known His name, to take part in its Passover Feast, and to nourish their faith at the altars of the fatherland.

In one of these homes, in Cyrene, a town on the north coast of Africa, a son was born, just as Saul was born in Tarsus, his intensely Jewish name, Simeon, declares his father's faith. He felt the fire of devotion burning in his bones when he came to manhood, and he turned his face towards the Holy City. "My feet shall stand within thy gates, O Jerusalem, whither the tribes go up, the tribes of the Lord, unto the testimony of Israel, to give thanks unto the name of the Lord." But like many more who thronged Jerusalem at the time of the Passover, he could find no dwelling-place within the city walls, and he sought out a lodging in the country. Morning by morning, just as Jesus did, he went his way into the city, and when the evening was come, he went out to his Bethany, and lodged there. The night before the day of Preparation, this devout Jew lay down in peace in his sweet country lodging-place, and he awoke in holy calm, and made his way through fields, gleaming with the scarlet anemones of spring, musical with the bleating of the lambs, to the Temple of God. His heart was filled with Passover gladness, but he did not know the things that awaited him there.

. . . Jesus comes forth bearing the two beams to make His cross. He must carry them to Calvary. But the true body and the reasonable soul of Jesus had spent their utmost strength. He who hungered and thirsted, who sat in weariness by the well, who fell asleep, outworn and weary in the midst of the storm, was led out of the judgment hall, utterly spent . . . What must it have been to bear the sin of men, and to know that the morning light would bring only a cross. It is no marvel that when its beams are placed upon Him, He finds its burden greater than He can bear. He staggers and sways, and falls. The soldiers look round for some one to take His place. They would not have borne the accursed wood for any criminal. They dared not lay hands on any priest, or suggest such an insult to one of the populace. Here is this stranger, who has pressed in through the crowd, and now looks on in pity at the sight. This unknown man, this pilgrim from the South, will serve the purpose. The soldiers' strong hands seize him, he is dragged from his standing-place in the crowd, the beams are laid upon his shoulders, and, with soldiers before and soldiers behind, within lines of flashing steel, Jesus and Simon march on—Simon of Cyrene bears the cross of Jesus.

—W. M. CLOW

See Him in Raiment Rent

See Him in raiment rent,
With His blood dyed:
Women walk sorrowing,

By His side.
Heavy that cross to Him,
Weary the weight:
One who will help Him stands
At the gate.
Multitudes hurrying
Pass on the road:
Simon is sharing with
Him the load.
Who is this traveling
With the curst tree—
This weary prisoner—
Who is He?
Follow to Calvary,
Tread where He trod:
This is the Lord of life—
Son of God.
Is there no loveliness—
You who pass by—
In that lone Figure which
Marks the sky?
You Who would love Him, stand,
Gaze at His face;
Tarry awhile in your
Worldly race.
As the swift moments fly
Through the blest week,
Jesus, in penitence,
Let us seek.
On the cross lifted up,
Thy face I scan,
Scarred by that agony—
Son of Man.
Thorns form Thy diadem,
Rough wood Thy throne,
To Thee Thy outstretched arms

Draw Thine own.
Nails hold Thy hands and feet,
While on Thy breast
Sinketh Thy bleeding head
Sore oppressed.
Loud is Thy bitter cry,
Rending the night,
As to Thy darkened eyes
Fails the light.
Shadows of midnight fall,
Though it is day;
Friends and disciples stand
Far away.
Loud scoffs the dying thief,
Mocking Thy woe;
Can this my Savior be
Brought so low?
Yes, see the title clear,
Written above,
"Jesus of Nazareth,"
Name of love!
What, O my Savior dear,
What didst Thou see,
That made Thee suffer and
Die for me?
Child of My grief and pain!
From realms above,
I came to lead thee to
Life and love.
For thee My blood I shed,
For thee I died;
Safe in thy faithfulness
Now abide.
I saw thee wandering,
Weak and at strife;
I am the Way for thee,

Truth and life.
Follow My path of pain,
Tread where I trod:
This is the way of peace
Up to God.
O I will follow Thee,
Star of my soul!
Through the great dark I press
To the goal.
Yes, let me know Thy grief,
Carry Thy cross,
Share in Thy sacrifice,
Gain Thy loss.
Daily I'll prove my love,
Through joy and woe;
Where Thy hands point the way,
There I go.
Lead me on year by year,
Safe to the end,
Jesus, my Lord, my Life,
King and Friend.

—EDWARD MONRO and MRS. M. DEARMER
From *The English Hymnal*

Man from Cyrene
(Excerpt)

He was big, this Jew—bigger than most men, his shoulders like a yoke; not clumsy, but lithe and powerful, with hands that could break a large animal's neck, arms that could swing two sacks of wheat with rhythmic grace, and a neck like the trunk of a rising cypress tree.

His face was broad and strong and friendly. When he laughed, as he often did, loudly and freely, his pitch-black beard parted as he threw back his massive head. He was dark, almost as dark as a Numidian. And so they called him Simon Niger. This did not disturb him. His heart was spacious—though a wrong word might cause his eyes to flame and his hands to tremble with resentful anger.

His eyes were calm, but deep within them lurked rebellion. His mouth was relaxed, but sometimes it could compress to a thin and angry line and his jaws clamp as if he were forcing far back within himself something that he dare not liberate.

> *Simon saw the thin hands of Jesus lying in the white dust of the footpath, with blood smears on the knuckles.*

He was barely forty. But his face was marked with crisscross lines, for he had known suffering—more of the body than of the spirit. He was a patriot who had been trodden beneath the heel of the Empire. He was a son of Israel, who, under Tiberius, was forced to breathe the poisoned air of Rome.

Two soldiers bent down to lift Jesus to his feet. "Leave him alone," the centurion ordered harshly. "He cannot carry the cross any further."

The centurion stood there in vexation, looking at Golgotha, which was not so far away, and back over the crowds to where the tower on Antonia shone dimly. He shuddered. He found all crucifixions an ordeal. Even if a murderer was involved, he shrank from the task of execution.

He saw the thin hands of Jesus lying in the white dust of the footpath, with blood smears on the knuckles. He looked away quickly.

He saw Simon Niger standing there—big, dark, powerful. The centurion looked intently at Simon, and he was impressed by the strength of this rustic Jew who, impelled by curiosity, had apparently joined them from some adjacent field. He could not stomach further trouble with this cross. They had been wasting time ever since they had placed the cross on the Nazarene's shoulder at Antonia. In a few hours it would be noon, and he did not want to be stuck at Golgotha till the late hours of night.

"You there—come here!" the centurion called to Simon and motioned to him with his sword to approach. Simon grew still, and his first impulse was to turn and flee. But when the centurion beckoned again with his sword, he walked slowly nearer. His eyes were narrowed, his whole body tensed.

A silence fell over the crowd. All that Simon was conscious of was the barking of the dog somewhere, the scarlet plumes of the soldiers, the glint of their helmets.

He stopped a few steps away from the centurion, his eyes filled with loathing and contempt. He felt the same animosity as on that evening in Cyrene when he confronted Vitellius. The centurion jerked his head in the direction of Jesus. "Come, carry the cross," he ordered Simon.

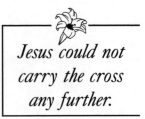

Jesus could not carry the cross any further.

Simon did not stir. There was a prickling sensation on his skin and a singing in his head. His breath felt warm within his nostrils. It seemed to him that he was floating in a vast, silent, empty space where nothing could touch him.

"I told you to carry the cross," the centurion commanded again. His steely eyes had become colder, and his chin jutted out from under his helmet.

"Let him carry his own cross," Simon said hoarsely. "Is he not a man of miracles?"

"I am not concerned with his miracles. All I know is that he cannot carry his cross any further. Come!"

"Look for one of his disciples. I am not one of them."

The centurion stared threateningly at the big Jew.

"You have a lot to say. Do not forget to whom you are talking."

"What I say is the truth."

"You are speaking to a Roman centurion."

"And you're speaking to a free Jew. Nobody can force me to carry this cross. I am only standing here as an onlooker."

"A Roman can compel a Jew to do anything he wishes."

Simon felt pulses beating in his head. The figure of the centurion grew hazy before him.

The crowds forgot about Jesus. They looked at the Jew and the Roman who stood so close to one another, anger the one link that bound them.

The centurion made a small movement with his sword. Simon was only vaguely conscious of the soldiers forming a circle round him, their spears and swords at the ready. He looked at Jesus lying in the dust, utterly exhausted. He looked completely defenseless, his hands limp and motionless, his narrow face reddened with his blood. Simon saw how his wounds had bled into his worn sandals.

Just like any human being . . . The man was only human.

"Where are your disciples? Why don't they carry your cross?" Simon shouted to the prisoner.

Jesus looked up at him, his eyes gentle but filled with pain. He looked pleadingly, as if he thirsted and was begging for water, at the big man

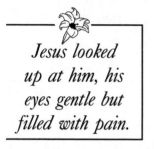

Jesus looked up at him, his eyes gentle but filled with pain.

who stood menacingly over him. Like any human being, and in pain . . .

But he spoke no word, only gazed at Simon. Simon felt as if the man were staring at him for all eternity. Then the slight body seemed to shudder, and Jesus looked off toward the Mount of Olives. His head fell forward again on his panting chest. His hands clenched with pain. His narrow shoulders moved, his face contorted—and Simon understood, for he had seen many men whom the Romans had scourged.

"You are a human being; you are no god. You are not even a prophet," Simon whispered angrily, and although he thought that Jesus had not heard, he looked up slowly and the pain had vanished from his eyes. There was only compassion there.

The big man still stood hesitating. He felt the point of a spear in his back—a small center of incipient pain. He heard the creaking of the soldiers' sandals. He heard their breathing. Then he felt, like the point of a heated arrow, another spear touch him, at the junction of his head and neck. Penetration here would bring immediate death.

"Pick up the cross," the centurion said again. His voice seemed to come from a remote place, like a message from the clouds.

Simon shuffled forward, stopped, and stared at the rough wood of the cross. He closed his eyes, seized the cross, and swung it up on his shoulders—swung it with so much vigor that a soldier who had come too close was knocked to the ground.

As he stood upright, he heard the mob's derision. "There goes his new disciple!" they shouted. He turned around, his head bent under the weight of the cross; and because they humiliated him, he spat freely at them. They shrieked with delight because he was helpless and looked grotesque beneath the cross.

—FRANS VENTER

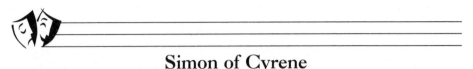

Simon of Cyrene

A Monologue taken from Mark 15:16–21.
No additional staging required.

Introduction

Simon of Cyrene is a figure who affords only one verse of scripture.

He was a faithful Jew living in Northern Africa.

Some speculate that he was black.

This is probably not true because one of his sons' name was Rufus (Red).

As a faithful Jew who had been scattered during the exile, he returned
to his homeland for the feast of the Passover.

Let us use our imagination.

Let's imagine we are in Africa when he returned to Cyrene to talk to his
two sons—Alexander and Rufus—about the things that happened
on his trip.

Let's realize that they are Jews—not Christians.

Remember also that we know the story of Jesus
but they had never heard it at all.

Simon speaks:

Boys, come sit down.

I just have to tell you what happened on my trip to Jerusalem.

The reason I'm home early is because I just had to hurry to tell you.

As you know, I didn't leave as early as I wanted.

You remember how nothing seemed to go right that morning as I packed to leave.

And, as you could expect, the more I hurried, the slower I got.

When I neared Jerusalem I was running way behind schedule.

I had missed so many things.

I knew that I had to hurry because I had to make housing arrangements—

which isn't easy during Passover.

You know how it is when you're hurrying—there are always problems.

This time the problem was a traffic jam.

I was not far from the place outside Jerusalem called "Golgotha"

because it looks like a skull.

Right ahead of me was a huge mob of people.

It looked like they might be watching a parade.

I had no time to wait so I pushed my way through the crowd.

When I got to the front of the crowd, I found myself next to the road.

There in the distance I could see a man trying to carry a cross.

He had been badly beaten.

Boys, I've seen lots of beatings but I've never seen one this bad before!

It was all he could do to carry his cross—in fact he would never have made it up to Golgotha.

I didn't know what to make of it.

But then I saw some people I recognized.

They were devout Jews.

I had met them on previous trips to Jerusalem.

I pushed my way over next to Ananias who was a Pharisee—

a very Godly man

and I asked him, "What is happening?"

He said, "This man thinks he is the son of God!"

That made me so mad, that I shouted in a loud voice and shook my hand . . .

"YOU BLASPHEMER!"

Ananias also said, "He calls himself the King of the Jews."

I couldn't control myself.

I shouted many things:

"YOU TRAITOR!

YOU HYPOCRITE!
YOU'RE GETTING EXACTLY WHAT YOU DESERVE . . . ."
As I continued to shout,
he and the soldiers were drawing near to me.
Right in the middle of my shouting,
and I guess I was just about out of my head,
one of the soldiers reached out and grabbed my
  arm.
This man had just fallen again.
The soldier said, "Carry this Cross!"
Well—I hated to carry that cross.
First of all I was late.
I didn't have time for interruptions.
Besides, he should have to do it himself.
Nevertheless, I had no choice.
So, with anger, impatience and many other emotions all worked up,
I bent over to pick up the cross.
Boys this was the magic moment.
As I picked up the cross I touched him.
His blood was spilled on me.
I don't know if I was crazy or not,
but I immediately remembered how our ancestors put the blood of the
  lamb
on their doorways and the children of the Israelites were spared.
Not only did I touch him and get his blood on me,
but as I bent over to put my shoulder under the cross,
our faces were only inches apart.
I saw his eyes!
I'll never forget that moment as long as I live.
For the first time I saw that he was not a violent man.
In his eyes I saw many things.
I saw that he had heard my screams just a few moments earlier.
I felt so guilty!
And yet his eyes seemed to say . . .
"God has forgiven you because you didn't know what you did."
His eyes forced love to flow from them.

> *The place of crucifixion outside Jerusalem was called "Golgotha" because it looks like a skull.*

It was like light from a flame.
It penetrated me and made me feel like I counted.
It made me forget myself.
No longer did I remember that I had a hurried
    schedule.
Somehow I felt like I was surrounded by love.
It's a funny feeling
It's like being in the presence of God himself!
Boys, I wish I were an artist.
I would paint a picture of that love in his eyes.

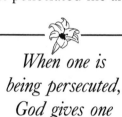

When one is being persecuted, God gives one extra strength.

It was so priceless and so valuable.
Yet he said I could show others the same love and the same power
because God would give it to me.
That's another thing.
He spoke to me all the way up the hill.
I felt that he was speaking only to me.
He was in great pain and suffering.
And yet he spoke in a calm voice.
I was the one who should have been comforting him,
but he was comforting me!
He told me that it is better to give your life for those you love
than to try to force them to change their ways.
He told me that when one is being persecuted
God gives us extra strength.
Then I asked him about my life.
You boys know that I have felt something was lacking.
I asked him about it and he said
that if I will give my life responding to the love of God
and showing it to others,
I will find what I lack.
I admit that I didn't know exactly what he meant
but I'm beginning to learn.
I know now that it's not enough to keep the laws,
because your importance is placed on the laws themselves.
But when you love people, your primary concern becomes people.

But boys, something else happened on that trip with the cross.
Somehow as I carried that cross
I got a taste of the suffering that was ahead for him.
I think I experienced a part of the suffering he had to endure.
I experienced pain.
I felt the pain of having nails driven through the body to the cross.
I felt the pains of the wounds of his beating.
I felt the struggle of fighting for that next breath on that cross.
But there was more than pain.
I felt his suffering of loneliness.
Boys, there is nothing as lonely as walking that hill

> *It's not enough to keep the laws, because the importance is placed on the laws themselves.*

with people shouting, and spitting, and throw-
ing rocks.
He was so lonely because his closest friends
had left him
and only watched from a distance.
But more important,
the loneliness was intensified by the hatred in the air.
You could feel it!
It was as if he was a scapegoat.
And they were killing him for their own sins.
While I carried that cross I knew this was for real.
This wasn't a game!
When I first began yelling at him, it was unreal.
I was yelling at a thing,
but after meeting him,
he was no longer a thing.
Once we begin picking the time for the cross,
then we'll start picking the size,
and then the weight,
and finally the convenience.
I have thought much on my way home
and realized when your mother was ill for so long . . . .
that was a cross we had to bear.

When the people in our synagogue began finding fault with each other
and with the Rabbi
and we found ourselves in the middle
That was our cross.

By the power of God Simon was able to help carry His cross.

When the fellow at work the other day was making fun of religion,
and of morality
and all those other things
This was my cross—that I might stand up for God.
There's another lesson.
When we carry our cross and run into trouble,
God gives us a helper.
That's what I was for Jesus.
If we are trying to carry the cross, that's all God can ask.
Let me say one last thing.
I know that by my sins,
I have helped kill Jesus.
But I also know that by the power of God
I have been able to help carry his cross.
You boys can help him carry his cross each day.
And if you'll do this you'll be ready
for that cross that will be placed on your shoulder unexpectedly.

Conclusion

Are you ready to bear your cross?
Must Jesus bear the cross alone,
and all the world go free?
No, there's a cross for everyone,
and there's a cross for me.

END

—LARRY R. LINVILLE

LARRY R. LINVILLE—Larry Linville wrote this Simon of Cyrene monologue as a sermon in the Spring of 1968 as he was graduating from
seminary school. He has preached it every year since to his apprecia-
tive parishioners. Larry is currently the pastor of McMurry United Meth-
odist Church in Claycomo, Missouri.

For Simon of Cyrene

The cross is too heavy for him; the sap is still in the wood. That young fellow passing by is vigorous. Let him carry it for the condemned man—not very far, now. A kindly-looking fellow, he carried another's cross, and has received the new message in his heart though he has never heard it with his ears. Thus in the last hour there comes a new disciple . . .

While the cross is thus borne forwards on a young man's powerful shoulders, there totters behind it the pale figure of the prophet, suddenly grown old, pushed and jostled by the soldiers of the escort.

Up there on the hill, more legionnaires are already at work, hammering and delving, for there are two other crucifixions today, Jews expiating the crimes of theft and murder. While some of the soldiers are digging holes in the ground, others are nailing the criminals to the crosses as these lie flat upon the soil. One of them resists; but strong hands hold him fast, his yells are ignored, and the huge nails are driven home, one through each hand, and one through both feet. Nail them firmly, so that no cord need be wasted on the malefactors! Now, up with the cross! . . . Thus almost simultaneously the two crosses with the thieves nailed to them are set up in the scorching sunlight, and the air is rent with the screams of the tortured men.

He whose turn is now to come sees all this as if in a dream. "Murderers and thieves," he thinks; "poor men, led astray, sentenced, and hurried off to their doom!" Above the head of each a placard has been affixed, declaring in three languages the nature of the offenders' crimes. There must be such a placard for him, too. Yes, that thickset little soldier, the one who had kicked him just now, is nailing it to his cross. "Rex Judaeorum." . . .

He suddenly becomes aware that his arms have been seized by pitiless hands, and that he has been stretched on the cross. He watches a nail, which looms gigantic before his eyes. Horror overwhelms him; pain racks him; he faints.

When he comes to his senses again, and grows aware of the fiery smart in his wounds, he turns his head to right and to left, and the sight of the other crosses recalls him to an understanding of what has happened.

Above the head of each thief a placard has been affixed, declaring the nature of the offenders' crimes.

As the slow minutes ebb away, pain chases pain through his tortured frame, as if it were being seared with fire, devoured by beasts of prey.

At length, when ages, as it seems, have passed, when he feels that the heart in his frail body is breaking; when intelligence and imagination are clouded, and faith and hope are obscured; when all his consciousness is filled with pain—he breaks the silence he has kept throughout these dreadful hours. The torment of mind and body finds vent in a heart-rending cry.

This cry of agony and despair ends a life which for thirty years has expressed itself in the gentle tones of love that brings solace to others, in the voiceless song of an affectionate human heart."

—EMIL LUDWIG
From *Behold the Man*

April 5—Morning

"On him they laid the cross, that he might bear it after Jesus."
—LUKE 23:26

We see in Simon's carrying the cross a picture of the work of the Church throughout all generations; he is the cross bearer after Jesus. Mark then, Christian, Jesus does not suffer so as to exclude your suffering. He bears a cross, not that you may escape it, but that you may endure it. Christ exempts you from sin, but not from sorrow. Remember that, and expect to suffer.

But let us comfort ourselves with this thought, that in our case, as in Simon's, it is not our cross, but Christ's cross which we carry. When you are molested for your piety; when your religion brings the trial of cruel mockings upon you, then remember it is not your cross, it is Christ's cross; and how delightful is it to carry the cross of our Lord Jesus!

You carry the cross after him. You have blessed company; your path is marked with the footprints of your Lord. The mark of his blood red shoulder is upon that heavy burden. 'Tis his cross, and he goes before you as a shepherd goes before his sheep. Take up your cross daily, and follow him.

Do not forget, also, that you bear this cross in partnership. It is the opinion of some that Simon only carried one end of the cross, and not the whole of it. That is very possible; Christ may have carried the heavier part, against the transverse beam, and Simon may have borne the lighter end. Certainly it is so with you; you do but carry the light end of the cross, Christ bore the heavier end.

> *When you are molested for your piety, just remember what a delight it is to carry the cross of Jesus!*

And remember, though Simon had to bear the cross for a very little while, it gave him lasting honour. Even so the cross we carry is only for a little while at most, and then we shall receive the crown, the glory. Surely we should love the cross, and, instead of shrinking from it, count it very dear, when it works out for us "a far more exceeding and eternal weight of glory."

—C. H. SPURGEON
From *Morning and Evening*

CHAPTER TWO

Golgotha: The Place of the Skull

CHAPTER · TWO

Golgotha: The Place of the Skull

MARK 15:22–23
²²*And they brought Him to the place Golgotha, which is translated, Place of a Skull.* ²³*Then they gave Him wine mingled with myrrh to drink, but He did not take it.*

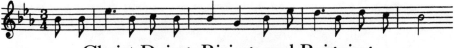

Christk Dying, Rising, and Reigning

He dies! the heav'nly Lover dies!
The Tidings strike a doleful Sound
On my poor Heart-strings: deep he lies
In the cold Caverns of the Ground.

Come, Saints, and drop a Tear or two
On the dear Bosom of your God,
He shed a Thousand Drops for you,
A thousand Drops of richer Blood.

Here's Love and Grief beyond degree,
The Lord of Glory dies for Men!
But lo, what sudden Joys I see!
JESUS the dead revives again.

The rising God forsakes the Tomb,
Up to his Father's Court he flies;

Cherubic Legions guard him home,
And shout him welcome to the Skies.

Break off your Tears, ye Saints, and tell
How high our Great Deliverer reigns;
Sing how he spoil'd the Hosts of Hell,
And led the Monster Death in Chains.

—ISAAC WATTS
From *Lyric Poems, Book 1*

ISAAC WATTS (1674–1748)—Known as the Father of Modern Hymnody, Isaac Watts had the gift of rhyme at an early age. When Watts was a child, his father was so annoyed at his constant rhyming that he began to whip poor Isaac. Even in his peril, Isaac couldn't stop. He cried out, "O father, do some pity take, and I will no more verses make!" Fortunately for us, he didn't stop. Watts eventually wrote over 600 hymns, many of which are commonly sung today.

Poem

Strong Sorrow-wrestler of Mount Calvary,
Speak through the blackness of Thine Agony,
Say, have I ever known Thee? Answer me!
Speak, Merciful and Mighty, lifted up
To draw those to Thee who have power to will
The roseate Baptism, and the bitter Cup,
The Royal Graces of the Cross-Crowned Hill,
Terrible Golgotha—among the bones
Which whiten thee, as thick as splintered stones
Where headlong rocks have crushed themselves away
I stumble on—Is it too dark to pray?

—D. B. DOLBEN

Untitled

Behold him, ye that pass by,
The bleeding Prince of life and peace!
Come, sinners, see your Maker die,
And say, was ever grief like his?
Come, feel with me his blood applied:
My Lord, my Love, is crucified.

Then let us sit beneath his cross,
And gladly catch the healing stream,
All things for him account but loss,
And give up all our hearts to him.
Of nothing think or speak beside:
My Lord, my Love, is crucified.

—CHARLES WESLEY

CHARLES WESLEY (1707–1788)—Charles Wesley wrote over 6,000 hymns. Unfortunately, his work was frequently altered which prompted him to include the following statement in the preface to one of his hymnals:

I beg to mention a thought which has been long upon my mind, and which I should long ago have inserted in the public papers, had I not been unwilling to stir up a nest of hornets. Many gentlemen have done my brother and me (though without naming us) the honour to reprint many of our hymns. Now they are perfectly welcome to do so, provided they print them just as they are. But I desire they would not attempt to mend them, for they are really not able. None of them is able to mend either the sense or the verse. Therefore, I must beg of them these two favours: either to let them stand just as they are, to take things for better or worse, or to add the true reading in the margin, or at the bottom of the page, that we nay no longer be accountable either for the nonsense or for the doggerel of other men.

Obsecration Before the Crucifix

Lord, by this sweet and saving sign,
Defend us from our foes and thine.
Jesus, by thy wounded feet,
Direct our path aright:
Jesus, by thy nailed hands,
Move ours to deeds of love:
Jesus, by thy pierced side,
Cleanse our desires:
Jesus, by thy crown of thorns,
Annihilate our pride:
Jesus, by thy silence,
Shame our complaints:
Jesus by thy parched lips,
Curb our cruel speech:
Jesus, by thy closing eyes,
Look on our sin no more:
Jesus, by thy broken heart,
Knit ours to thee.
And by this sweet and saying sign,
Lord, draw us to our peace and thine.

—RICHARD CRASHAW
From *Complete Poetry*

Lion and Lamb
(Excerpt)

Such was the life of Jesus on earth. The Gospels tell of a man who was cut off in the flower of His age, His work destroyed just when it should have taken root, His friends scattered, His honor broken, His name a laughingstock. In the words of Isaiah, He was "a worm and not a man, a thing despised and rejected by men, a man of sorrows and familiar with suffering," who experienced the nadir of agony such as no other man or woman dreamed of. No one has ever died as Jesus died because He was life itself. No one was ever punished for sin as He was—the sinless One. No one ever plunged down into the vacuum of evil as did Jesus of Nazareth. Who will ever know the excruciating pain behind His words, "My Father, why have You abandoned Me?"

This is the New Testament picture of Jesus—the suffering servant, a man who lives as a lackey and dies in disgrace. He is spurned, avoided, treated as a leper, a born loser. He is one stricken by God, publicly beaten, whipped by disgusted, righteous society. Eliminate Him, they say, He is distasteful. Drive Him across the tracks, out of town, out of society. He is roughly handled, pushed around, taken out, killed, and buried among evildoers.

Jesus resonated with the depths of human sorrow. He became lost with the lost, hungry with the hungry, and thirsty with the thirsty. On the Cross He journeyed to the far reaches of loneliness, so that He could be lonely with those who are lonely and rob loneliness of its killing power by sharing it Himself.

—BRENNAN MANNING

Poem

Am I a stone, and not a sheep,
   That I can stand, O Christ, beneath Thy cross,
   To number drop by drop Thy Blood's slow loss,
And yet not weep?

Not so those women loved
   Who with exceeding grief lamented Thee;
   Not so fallen Peter weeping bitterly;
   Not so the thief was moved;

Not so the Sun and Moon
 Which hid their faces in a starless sky,
 A horror of great darkness at broad noon—
I, only I.

Yet give not o'er,
 But seek Thy sheep, true Shepherd of the flock;
 Greater than Moses, turn and look once more
And smite a rock.

—CHRISTINA ROSSETTI

Pilate

Almost added to his titles:
Savior of the Savior of the World;
But he washed his hands.

The judge being judged
Found no fault;
But they took Him away to be crucified.

Who could know?
Replies were in other mouths,
Truth remained mute in noisy assembly.

At last, truth could not be worded,
It bore an act.
History was impregnated.

Pilate asked about truth,
Then pronounced sentence,

Washed his hands,
And waited
And waited
To see what happened.

—BERNARD S. VIA, JR.
From *Seasons of Faith*

Basic Christianity
(*Excerpt*)

Christ died once for all. The Son of God identified himself with the sins of men. He was not content to take our nature upon him; he took our iniquity upon him as well. He was not only 'made flesh' in the womb of Mary; he was 'made sin' on the cross of Calvary. God refused to impute our sins to us, or count them against us. That is, in his utterly undeserved love for us, he would not make us answerable for our own sins. Jesus Christ, the lamb of God, had no sins of his own; he was made sin with our sins, on the cross.

—JOHN STOTT

The Cross

I saw a cross of burning gold
And jewels glorious to behold;
Over it a golden crown,
All the people falling down.
I saw an ugly cross of wood,
On it there were stains of blood;
Over it a crown of thorn,
Plaited for the people's scorn.

Cross of gold, no fruit was thine,
Nothing but the empty shrine.
Cross of wood, thou living tree,
The true vine clung fast to thee.

—MARY E. COLERIDGE

The Parable of Joy
(Excerpt)

The morning had not gone well for either of them. All Pilate wanted was to be rid of the noisy, troublemaking Jews. Jesus, too, seemed to want it all to be over.

They had been dragging him from place to place since His arrest in the garden. He had been struck with rods, He had been slapped in the face, blindfolded, and spat upon. They had dressed Him up in robes and horse blankets. They had woven a crown of thorns and pressed it down on his head. It was supposed to be a joke, but no one laughed when they saw him with the blood dripping down His cheeks.

Pilate felt as if Jesus would have forgiven him for what he had done to Him so far.

Pilate turned without a word and went back into the palace. Jesus followed dutifully behind him.

"Where did you come from?" he asked as he looked intently into Jesus' bloody face. He asked as if he were expecting to hear the answer "heaven."

By now this all seemed useless to Jesus, who knew exactly what was before Him. His eyes slowly closed as if He were about to faint.

"What is the matter with you!" Pilate screamed two inches from his face. "I could free you; I have the power. Or I could let the mob have their way and have you nailed to a cross." He threatened Jesus like a schoolyard bully.

Jesus, in pain and exhaustion, whispered, "You have no power, only what has been given to you from heaven. The ones outside are more guilty than you."

It was remarkable to Pilate that Jesus spoke with no bitterness. He felt as if Jesus would have forgiven him for what he had done to Him so far—if Pilate had had it in himself to ask for forgiveness.

—MICHAEL CARD

The Lion, the Witch, and the Wardrobe
(Excerpt)

"It means," said Aslan, "that though the Witch knew the Deep Magic, there is a magic deeper still which she did not know. Her knowledge goes back only to the dawn of Time. But if she could have looked a little further back, into the stillness and darkness before Time dawned, she would have read there a different incantation. She would have known that when a willing victim who had not committed treachery was killed in a traitor's stead, the Table would crack and Death itself would start working backwards."

—C. S. LEWIS

Timeless

Ah Jesus!
The centuries will not let me forget,
And two thousand years
Are but as yesterday.
The scraping sound of a cross over Jerusalem's cobblestones
Is a pulse beat;

And blood still gushes in a cruel world
That wars on.

—BERNARD S. VIA, JR.
From *Seasons of Faith*

Who Is This?
(Excerpt)

The cross of itself was but a rugged piece of wood, the "symbol of suffering and shame." Of itself it had no power to save. Not the cross, but the Christ of the cross, is our hope of redemption, for "God was in Christ, reconciling the world unto himself" (2 Cor. 5:19). The significance of the cross, then, is a Person, and the significance of that Person was in his office as our Mediator.

Yes, Jesus must die as a king. A King represented his people. Jesus had to work Pilate, as he did Caiaphas, to get the correct charge to which he must plead guilty. He must die as a spiritual king or Messiah.

Furthermore, it was customary under Roman jurisprudence to place a sign over the cross of execution, signifying for what crime the victim was being executed. Over Jesus' cross Pilate wrote in Hebrew, Greek, and Latin the superscription, "THIS IS JESUS THE KING OF THE JEWS" (Matt. 27:37). The Jewish rulers protested, but to no avail. Jesus died as a king!

—HERSCHEL H. HOBBS

O Sacred Head, Now Wounded

O sacred Head, now wounded,
With grief and shame weighed down;
Now scornfully surrounded
With thorns, Thine only crown;

O sacred Head, what glory,
What bliss till now was Thine!
Yet, though despised and gory,
I joy to call Thee mine.

What Thou, my Lord, hast suffered
Was all for sinners' gain,
Mine, mine was the trangression,
But Thine the deadly pain.
Lo, here I fall, my Savior!
'Tis I deserve Thy place;
Look on me with Thy favor,
Vouchsafe to me Thy grace.

What language shall I borrow
To thank Thee, dearest Friend;
For this Thy dying sorrow,
Thy pity without end?
O make me Thine forever;
And should I fainting be,
Lord, let me never, never
Outlive my love to Thee.

—Attributed to BERNARD
OF CLAIRVAUX

BERNARD OF CLAIRVAUX (1090–1153)—In 1112, Bernard entered the Cistercian abbey of Centeaux, taking along four or five brothers and nearly 25 friends, and began his remarkable life as a monk. After the abbey of Centeaux became overcrowded, Bernard led a group to found a house at Clairvaux. He remained there as an abbot all his life, despite many efforts to elevate him to higher ecclesiastical office, thus establishing him as Bernard of Clairvaux. A holy life, a reputation for miraculous cures, and unusual eloquence made Bernard known far and wide, and soon, he became the most powerful religious influence in France and in all Western Europe. Through his writings, St. Bernard exerted a profound influence on Roman Catholic spirituality. His deep devotion to the Virgin Mary and to the infant Jesus is evident in his work, which consists of about 330 sermons, 500 known letters, and 13 treatises. His strong and eloquent style, intensely personal and direct, and full of Biblical allusions, has earned him the name "Doctor of the Church."

The Jesus I Never Knew
(Excerpt)

Even after watching scores of movies on the subject, and reading the Gospels over and over, I still cannot fathom the indignity, the *shame* endured by God's Son on earth, stripped naked, flogged, spat on, struck in the face, garlanded with thorns. Jewish leaders as well as Romans intended the mockery to parody the crime for which the victim had been condemned. *Messiah, huh? Great, let's hear a prophecy.* Wham. *Who hit you, huh?* Thunk. *C'mon, tell us, spit it out, Mr. Prophet. For a Messiah, you don't know much, do you?*

> God has shown self-restraint throughout history, allowing the Genghis Khans and the Hitlers and the Stalins to have their way.

You say you're a king? Hey, Captain, get a load of this. We have us a regular king here, don't we. Well, then, let's all kneel down before hizzoner. What's this? A king without a crown? Oh, that will never do. Here, Mr. King, we'll fix you a crown, we will . . .

It went like that all day long, from the bullying game of Blind Man's Bluff in the high priest's courtyard, to the professional thuggery of Pilate's and Herod's guards, to the catcalls of spectators turned out to jeer the criminals stumbling up the long road to Calvary, and finally to the cross iself where Jesus heard a stream of taunts from the ground below and even from the cross alongside. *You call yourself a Messiah? Well, then come down from that cross. How you gonna save us if you can't even save yourself?*

I have marveled at, and sometimes even openly questioned, the self-restraint God has shown throughout history, allowing the Genghis Khans and the Hitlers and the Stalins to have their way. But nothing—nothing compares to the self-restraint shown that dark Friday in Jerusalem. With every lash of the whip, every fibrous crunch of fist against flesh, Jesus must have mentally replayed the Temptation in the wilderness and in Gethsemane. Legions of angels awaited his command. One word, and the ordeal would end.

No theologian can adequately explain the nature of what took place within the Trinity on that day at Calvary. All we have is a cry of pain from a child who felt forsaken. We are not told what God the Father cried out at that moment. We can only imagine. The Son became "a curse for us," said Paul in Galatians, and "God made him who had no sin to be sin for us," he wrote the Corinthians. We know how God feels about sin; the sense of abandonment likely cut both ways.

—PHILIP YANCEY

The Head That Once Was Crowned with Thorns

The head that once was crowned with thorns
Is crowned with glory now;
A royal diadem adorns
The mighty Victor's brow.
The highest place that heaven affords
Is His, is His by right,
The King of kings, the Lord of lords,
And heaven's eternal light.
The Joy of all who dwell above,
The Joy of all below
To whom He manifests His love,
And grants His name to know.
To them the cross with all its shame,
With all its grace is giv'n,
Their name an everlasting name,
Their joy the joy of heav'n.

—THOMAS KELLY

The Final Week of Jesus
(Excerpt)

Jesus could have used the spectacular to get their attention. Why didn't he? Why didn't he stun them with a loop-a-dee-loop or a double backflip off the temple? When they demanded, "Crucify him!" why didn't he make their noses grow? Why is the miraculous part of Christ quiet this week? Why doesn't he do something spectacular?

No angelic shield protected his back from the whip. No holy helmet shielded his brow from the thorny crown. God crawled neck deep into the mire of humanity, plunged into the darkest cave of death, and emerged—alive.

Even when he came out, he didn't show off. He just walked out. Mary thought he was a gardener. Thomas had to have hands-on (or hands-in) proof. Jesus still ate, he still talked, he still broke bread with the Emmaus-bound disciples.

Do you see the point?

God calls us in a real world. He doesn't communicate by performing tricks.

In the final week those who demanded miracles got none and missed the one. They missed the moment in which a grave for the dead became the throne of a king.

—MAX LUCADO

And Can It Be?
(Stanzas 1, 2, 3 & 6)

And can it be, that I should gain
An interest in the Savior's blood?
Died he for me?—who caused his pain!

For me?—who him to death pursued.
Amazing love! how can it be
That thou, my God, shouldst die for me?

'Tis mystery all! Th'Immortal dies!
Who can explore his strange design?
In vain the first-born seraph tries
To sound the depths of Love divine.
'Tis mercy all! Let earth adore;
Let angel minds inquire no more.

He left his Father's throne above,
(So free, so infinite his grace!)
Emptied himself of all but love,
And bled for Adam's helpless race:
'Tis mercy all, immense and free!
For, O my God! it found out me!

No condemnation now I dread,
Jesus, and all in him, is mine:
Alive in him, my living Head,
And clothed in righteousness divine,
But I approach th'eternal throne,
And claim the crown, through Christ, my own.

—CHARLES WESLEY

Good Friday

If faith has its way
Today the world becomes Calvary,
A grappling place of death and life
Where evil tears at good
And flesh gives way.

Planet Calvary
Orbits a darkening sun
And dirties God with blood and bark
And the sullied profanities
Of men trying to forget what they do.

If faith has its way
Today the world becomes Calvary.

—BERNARD S. VIA, JR.
From *Seasons of Faith*

There Is a Green Hill Far Away

There is a green hill far away,
Without a city wall,
Where the dear Lord was crucified,
Who died to save us all.
We may not know, we cannot tell
What pains He had to bear;
But we believe it was for us
He hung and suffered there.
He died that we might be forgiven;
He died to make us good,
That we might go at last to heaven,
Saved by his precious blood.
O dearly, dearly has He loved,
And we must love Him too,
And trust in His redeeming love,
And try His works to do.

—CECIL F. ALEXANDER

Man of Sorrows! What a Name

Man of Sorrows! What a name
For the Son of God who came,
Ruined sinners to reclaim,
Hallelujah, what a Savior!
Bearing shame and scoffing rude,
In my place condemned He stood,
Sealed my pardon with His blood;
Hallelujah, what a Savior!
Guilty, vile and helpless we,
Spotless Lamb of God was He;
Full atonement! Can it be?
Hallelujah, what a Savior!
Lifted up was He to die,
"It is finished," was His cry;
Now in heaven exalted high,
Hallelujah, what a Savior!
When he comes, our glorious King,
All His ransomed home to bring,
Then anew this song we'll sing,
Hallelujah, what a Savior!

—PHILIP P. BLISS

PHILIP P. BLISS (1838–1876)—Philip Bliss might not have been known for his music. He grew up in farming communities in Pennsylvania and Ohio, and had little experience with "culture." He was ten years old before he ever heard a piano! After pursuing a career in education, Bliss attended a singing school for the first time. His voice developed into a beautiful bass and in 1860, he began teaching music and composing. After meeting D. L. Moody, he teamed up with Major D. W. Whittle and conducted revival meetings all over the country. Tragically, at the tender age of 38, he and his wife were killed in a train accident.

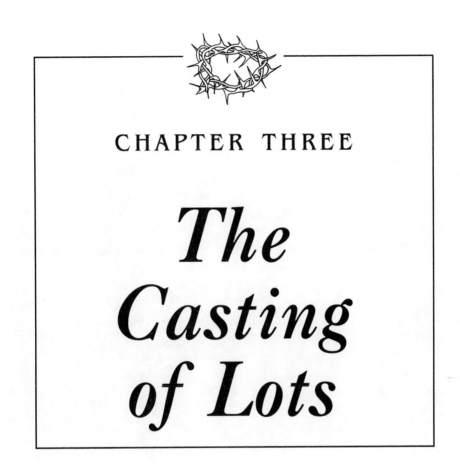

CHAPTER THREE

The Casting of Lots

CHAPTER · THREE

The Casting of Lots

LUKE 23:34–35
34Then Jesus said, "Father, forgive them, for they do not know what they do." And they divided His garments and cast lots. 35And the people stood looking on. But even the rulers with them sneered, saying, "He saved others; let Him save Himself if He is the Christ, the chosen of God."

The Crucifixion

"I miles, expedi crucem" (Go, soldier, get ready the cross"). In some such formula of terrible import Pilate must have given his final order. It was now probably about nine o'clock, and the execution followed immediately upon the judgment. The time required for the necessary preparation would not be very long, and during this brief pause the soldiers, whose duty it was to see that the sentence was carried out, stripped Jesus of the scarlet war-cloak, now dyed with the yet deeper stains of blood, and they laid it—or possibly only one of the beams of it—upon His shoulders, and led Him to the place of punishment.

The three crosses were laid on the ground. Then He was stripped naked of all His clothes, and then followed the most awful moment of all. He was laid down upon the implement of torture. He arms were stretched along the crossbeams, and at the center of the open palms the point of a huge iron nail was placed, and, by the blow of a mallet, was driven home into the wood.

In order to prevent the possibility of any rescue, even at the last moment—since instances had been known of men taken from the cross and restored to life—four soldiers with their centurion were left on the ground to guard the cross. The clothes of the victims always fell as booty to the men who had to perform so weary and disagreeable an office. Little dreaming how exactly they were fulfilling the mystic intimations of olden Jewish prophecy, they proceeded, therefore, to divide between them the garments of Jesus. The robe they tore into four parts, probably ripping it down the seams (Deut. Xxii, 12); but the under garment was formed of one continuous woven texture, and to tear would have been to spoil it; they therefore contented themselves with letting it become the property of any one of the four to whom it should fall by lot. When this had been decided, they sat down and watched Him till the end, beguiling the weary lingering hours by eating and drinking, and joking, and playing dice.

—FREDERIC WILLIAM FARRAR
From *The Life of Christ*

Gambler

And sitting down they watched him there,
The soldiers did;
There, while they played with dice,
He made his sacrifice,
And died upon the cross to rid
God's world of sin.
He was a gambler, too, my Christ,
He took his life and threw
It for a world redeemed.
And ere his agony was done,
Before the westering sun went down.
Crowning that day with crimson crown,
He knew that he had won.

—G. A. STUDDERT-KENNEDY
From *Christ in Poetry*

G. A. STUDDERT-KENNEDY (1883–1929)—Geoffrey Studdert-Kennedy entered the ministry in 1904. After becoming the vicar of a church, the outbreak of World War I prompted him to volunteer his services as a chaplain. He was quickly nicknamed Woodbine Willie because of his habit of passing out Woodbine-brand cigarettes to troops. He was well respected for his bravery under fire and was seen many times running to the front lines to aid the wounded and dying, which often included German soldiers. After the war, he worked with the Industrial Christian Fellowship, ministering to the homeless and unemployed all over Britain. It was said that "women wept and men broke down" at his sermons. As a mark of respect and love at his funeral, people placed packets of Woodbine cigarettes on his coffin and his grave.

The Greatest Story Ever Told
(Excerpt)

Calmly He hung there, suspended, as the guards who had nailed Him up threw dice for His robe which was without seam, woven from the top throughout. They had taken all His garments and divided them into four parts—one for each soldier. But when they looked at that beautiful seamless robe one of them proposed: "Let's not tear it. Let's cast lots for it, whose it shall be."

It was while the soldiers were throwing the dice that Jesus looked down and saw that He was not alone. Moving slowly forward through the crowd, coming ever closer to the cross, were three women—three Marys close at hand. Mary, His mother, stood at the foot of the cross. And Mary, the wife of Cleophas, His mother's sister, knelt beside her; Mary of Magdalene, out of whom he had cast seven devils, was prostrate on earth.

—FULTON OURSLER

FULTON OURSLER (1893–1952)—Many people are unaware that Fulton Oursler, in addition to being a renowned editor and writer, was also an amateur magician. One of his best-known works was *The Greatest Story Ever Told*, but he also penned an interesting book titled *Spirit Mediums Exposed* under the name Samri Frikell.

His Garments

He gave his life upon a cross;
To those who hung him there
He gave forgiveness—and he left
His clothes for them to wear!

That seamless vesture from whose hem
Heaven's healing power stole
Was worn above a Roman heart!
Oh, was that heart made whole?

Each hand that smote the thorn-crowned head,
Each arm that drove a nail,
He covered with his raiment fair,
And blood drops for them fell.

Was it I who pierced Thy side, my God,
And looked upon Thee there?
White garments from Thy stainless life
Oh give me, Lord, to wear!

—ESTHER LLOYD HAGG
From *Christ in Poetry*

Moments with the Savior
(Excerpt)

"Father, forgive them—"

The three words impale them as forcefully as the three spikes they used to impale him. They all look up, transfixed, as Jesus finishes his prayer.

"—for they do not know what they are doing."

Not only does Jesus ask his Father to forgive them, he offers a kind word on their behalf, explaining their behavior.

The calloused ears of these soldiers have heard all kinds of words on that hill. All kinds. And in every language. But they have never heard words like these. Never like these. Not once.

Until now.

A chasm of silence opens between the men, separating them from each other. An awkward moment for men used to loud talk and course language. In the quiet of that moment Jesus closes his eyes.

The silence below him is bridged by a few feeble planks of conversation. "What about his tunic?" asks one. "A shame to cut it up," says another. "Worth more in one piece."

The garment perhaps was woven by his mother. And if not by her, at least by somebody who loved him. The soldiers value it because it is seamless, not because it is his or because of the labor of love that it is.

And so dice are pulled from a pocket. "Winner takes all." A circle forms. After a few rolls they seem back to their old selves. The losers cursing. The winner bragging.

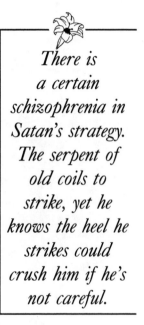

There is a certain schizophrenia in Satan's strategy. The serpent of old coils to strike, yet he knows the heel he strikes could crush him if he's not careful.

As the soldiers return to their stations, Satan returns to his. He is more cunning this time around. Instead of coming out in the open, he voices his temptations through the traffic of onlookers passing by the cross. They are his mouthpiece, sounding almost as an echo from those windswept hills in the wilderness three and a half years ago.

There is a certain schizophrenia in Satan's strategy. The serpent of old coils to strike, yet he knows the heel he strikes could crush him if he's not careful. He delights in seeing God's Son suffer, yet he fears what that suffering could accomplish.

—KEN GIRE

Mary's Song

I remember the night that Gabriel came
And told me all about you,
And I remember the night that you were born
And angels sang around you,
And the people came from far and near
And claimed you as their king
But to me
You were just my baby.

I still hear the anguished cry of mothers
When the soldiers came,
And we had to flee like fugitives,
And for years we hid away.
I watched you play out in the fields
With other boys and girls,
And for awhile
You were just my baby.

I've seen you heal the sick,
I've seen you make the lame walk
You've healed the blind, let deaf men hear,
And made the speechless talk.
Some people worshiped at your feet,
And some people spat on you.
I know you are the Son of God,
But you're my baby too.

Now here you are, with nails in your feet
A crown of thorns upon your head,
You call to them for water,
They bring you vinegar instead,

They're casting lots, for your clothes,
A Son of God they don't understand,
But can't they see,
That you're my baby.

Father in Heaven, I've done everything
That you have asked of me.
Please take care
Of my baby.

—ANNA MARIA JUNUS
From One Great Family website

The Crucifixion and the Resurrection

They struck him over the head with the stick, spat at him, and knelt down and pretended to do homage to him. Of course in a time when one emperor, Augustus, in his shows, had set ten thousand men to fighting each other to death to entertain the Roman public, life counted for very little. When the soldiers had finished making sport of him, they took off the purple cloak and put his own clothes back on him, and set out with him for the place of crucifixion.

Even in our days of new and refined cruelties, crucifixion is so brutal and cruel as hardly to bear description. Jesus was stripped of his clothes; his hands were nailed to the crossbeam. It was then raised and fastened to the upright, which was not as tall as Christian art has represented it. A peg between his thighs partly supported his body. His feet were then fastened with nails to the upright, and he was left to die of exhaustion and hunger, which might last for days. The proceedings before Pilate had been so hurried that it was only nine o'clock when he was put to the cross. The squad of soldiers were entitled to his clothes, as their perquisites for their work, and after dividing them by lot they, with the centurion in charge, sat down to keep watch, and see that no one tried to release him. They also hung the customary placard or piece of board above his head, with his name and his crime chalked on it. It read, "The king of the Jews."

—EDGAR J. GOODSPEED
From *A Life of Jesus*

EDGAR J. GOODSPEED (1871–1962)—The Bond Chapel at the University of Chicago Divinity School is the home of beautiful stained-glass windows that were donated to the chapel by Edgar J. Goodspeed, in memory of his wife, Elfleda, who died in 1949. Goodspeed graduated from Denison University in Ohio in 1890, and was one of nine Biblical scholars who worked on the Revised Standard Version of the Bible, which was published in 1946.

Good Friday

"The Son of God am I," he humbly said,
   And yet his torturers believed him not.
They taunted, scourged, and spat upon their Lord,
   And took possession of his clothes by lot.

They crucified him—watched him as he died;
   And long before his blood dried on the sod,
When nature turbulently voiced its ire,
   They fearfully admitted: He is God.

—ALICE B. JURICA
From *Christ in Poetry*

Casting of Lots

The casting of lots was a custom or rite used in ancient times to make important decisions, much as we practice drawing straws or flipping a coin today. Several examples of this practice occur in both the Old and New Testaments.

Lots were cast by the high priest to select the scapegoat on the Day of Atonement. (Lev. 18:8–10). This method was also used to divide the land of Canaan after its conquest under Joshua (Num. 26:55; Josh. 14:2). Lots were cast to select warriors to fight against the men of Gibeah (Judg. 20:9, 10) and apparently to choose Saul as the first king of Israel (1 Sam. 10:19–21). Sailors on the ship bound for Tarshish with Jonah on board used lots to determine who had caused the stormy seas (Jon. 1:7).

In the New Testament, Roman soldiers cast lots for Jesus' garments (Matt. 27:35). After prayer, the apostles used lots to choose Matthias as successor to Judas (Acts 1:24–26).

We can only speculate about what materials were used in the casting of lots. Some scholars believe several stones, or perhaps precious gems, were cast from a clay jug. Others connect the practice with Urim and Thummin, precious stones that were on, by, or in the breastplate of the high priest of Israel. The high priest used these stones in making important decisions, but it is not known exactly how this was done (Ex. 28:30).

"The lot is cast into the lap; but the whole disposing thereof is of the Lord."

Proverbs 16:33 demonstrates above that casting lots was not considered magic, because the decision was from the Lord. Despite this,

Sailors on the ship bound for Tarshish with Jonah on board used lots to determine who had caused the stormy seas.

there seems to be little justification for this practice today. Since the coming of God's Holy Spirit at Pentecost, we have had this ever-present resource to guide us in our decision making. As enlightened believers, we are urged to bring our needs to the Father in prayer and rely on the direction of the Holy Spirit.

—From *The Thomas Nelson Open Bible Study Notes*

Death and Burial

As the crucifiers proceeded with their awful task, not unlikely with roughness and taunts, for killing was their trade and to scenes of anguish they had grown callous through long familiarity. The agonized Sufferer, void of resentment but full of pity for their heartlessness and capacity for cruelty, voiced the first of the seven utterances delivered from the cross. In the spirit of God-like mercy He prayed: "Father, forgive them; for they know not what they do." Let us not attempt to fix the limits of the Lord's mercy; that it would be extended to all who in any degree could justly come under the blessed boon thereof ought to be a sufficing fact. There is significance in the form in which this merciful benediction was expressed. Had the Lord said, "I forgive you," His gracious pardon may have been understood to be but a remission of the cruel offense against Himself as One tortured under unrighteous condemnation; but the invocation of the Father's forgiveness was a plea for those who had brought anguish and death to the Father's Well Beloved Son, the Savior and Redeemer of the world. Moses forgave Miriam for her offense against himself as her brother; but God alone could remit the penalty and remove the leprosy that had come upon her for having spoken against Jehovah's high priest.

> *Let us not attempt to fix the limits of the Lord's mercy; that it would be extended to all who in any degree could justly come under the blessed boon thereof ought to be a sufficing fact.*

It appears that under Roman rule, the clothes worn by a condemned person at the time of execution became the perquisites of the executioners. The four soldiers in charge of the cross upon which the Lord suffered distributed parts of His raiment among themselves; and there remained His coat, which was a godly garment, woven throughout in one piece, without seam. To rend it would be to spoil; so the soldiers cast lots to determine who should have it; and in this circumstance the Gospel-writers saw a fulfillment of the psalmist's prevision: "They parted my garments among them, and upon my vesture did they cast lots."

—JAMES E. TALMAGE
From *Jesus the Christ*

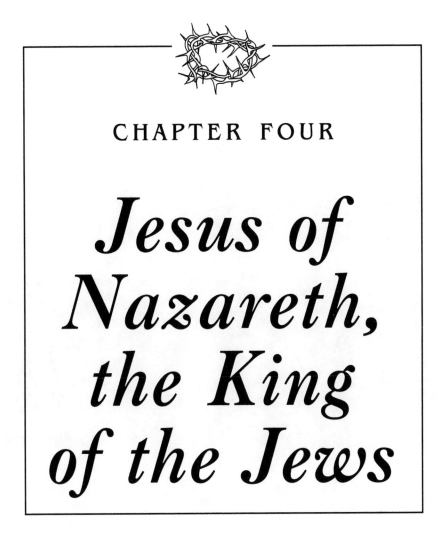

CHAPTER FOUR

Jesus of Nazareth, the King of the Jews

Jesus of Nazareth, the King of the Jews

JOHN 19:19–22

¹⁹Now Pilate wrote a title and put it on the cross. And the writing was: JESUS OF NAZARETH, THE KING OF THE JEWS. ²⁰Then many of the Jews read this title, for the place where Jesus was crucified was near the city; and it was written in Hebrew, Greek, and Latin. ²¹Therefore the chief priests of the Jews said to Pilate, "Do not write, 'The King of the Jews,' but, 'He said, "I am the King of the Jews."'" ²²Pilate answered, "What I have written, I have written."

Ave Crux, Spes Unica!

More than two crosses stand on either side
The Cross today on more than one dark hill;
More than three hours a myriad of men have cried,
And they are crying still.

Before Him now no mocking faces pass;
Heavy on all who built the cross, it lies;
Pilate is hanging there, and Caiaphas,
Judas without his price.

Men scourge each other with their stinging whips;
To crosses high they nail, and they are nailed;
More than one dying man with parched lips,
"My God! My God!" has wailed.

Enlarged is Golgotha. But One alone
His healing shadow over all can fling;
One King Divine has made His Cross a Throne.
"Remember us, O King!"

—EDWARD SHILLITO
From *Masterpieces of Religious Verse*

EDWARD SHILLITO (1872–1948)—In one of his best-known poems, Edward Shillito put himself in the place of a soldier and reflected on the sufferings of Christ and the soldier's role in helping us to believe in Him. During and after World War I, Shillito's work was collected into two books of religious poetry. Shillito's poetry was strongly influenced by the sufferings of young men being sent to fight in the war.

April 7—Morning

"O ye sons of men, how long will ye turn my glory into shame?"
—PSALM 4:2

An instructive writer has made a mournful list of the honours which the blinded people of Israel awarded to their long-expected King. (1.) They gave Him *a procession of honour,* in which Roman legionaries, Jewish priests, men and women, took a part, He Himself bearing His cross . . . (2.) They presented Him with *the wine of honour* . . . (3.) He was provided with *a guard of honour,* who showed their esteem of Him by gambling over His garments, which they had seized as their booty . . . (4.) *A throne of honour* was found for Him upon the bloody tree; no easier place of rest would rebel men yield to their liege Lord. The cross was, in fact, the full expression of the world's feeling towards Him; "There," they seemed to say, "Thou Son of God, this is the manner in which God Himself should be treated, could we reach Him." (5.) *The title of honour* was nominally "King of the Jews," but that the blinded nation distinctly repudiated, and really called Him "King of thieves," by preferring Barabbas, and by placing Jesus in the place of highest shame between two thieves. His glory was thus in all things turned into shame by the sons of men, but it shall yet gladden the eyes of saints and angels, world without end.

—C. H. SPURGEON
From *Morning & Evening*

Sermon 27

Of the signal Providence, which directed and ordered the Title affixed to the cross of Christ.

—LUKE 23:38

And a superscription also was written over him in letters of Greek, and Latin, and Hebrew, THIS IS THE KING OF THE JEWS.

Before I pass on to the Manner of Christ's death, I shall consider the title affixed to the cross; in which very much of the wisdom of Providence was discovered. It was the manner of the Romans, that the equity of their proceedings might the more clearly appear to the people, when they crucified any man, to publish the cause of his death, in a table written in capital letters, and placed over the head of the crucified. And that there might be at least a show and face of justice in Christ's death, he also shall have his title or superscription.

The worst and most unrighteous actions labour to cover and shroud themselves under pretension of equity. Sin is so shameful a thing, that it cares not to own its name. Christ shall have a table written for him also. This writing one evangelist calls the Accusation, "aitia", Matth. 27:37. Another calls it the Title, "titlos", John 19:19. Another the Inscription or Superscription, "epigrafe", so the text. And another the Superscription of his Accusations, "epigrafe tes aitias", Mark 15:26. In short, it was a fair legible writing, intended to express the fact or crime, for which the person died.

This was their usual manner, though sometimes we find it was published by the voice of the common crier. As in the case of Attalus the martyr, who was led about the amphitheatre, one proclaiming before him, this is Attalus the Christian. But it was customary and usual to express the crime in a written table, as the text expresses it. Wherein these three things offer themselves to your consideration.

First, The character or description of Christ, contained in that writing. And he is described by his kingly dignity: This is the king of the Jews. The very office, which but a little before, they had reproached and derided, bowing the knee to him in mockery, saying, Hail King of the Jews: the Providence of God so orders it, that therein he shall be vindicated and honoured. This is the King of the Jews: Or, as the other evangelists complete it, This is Jesus of Nazareth the King of the Jews.

> *Christ is described by his kingly dignity: This is the king of the Jews.*

Secondly, The person that drew his character or title. It was Pilate; he that but now condemned him: he that was his judge, shall be his herald, to proclaim his glory. For the title is honourable. Surely, this was not from himself, for he was Christ's enemy; but rather that Christ should want a tongue to clear him, the tongue of an enemy shall do it.

Thirdly, The time when this honour was done him: It was when he was at the lowest ebb of his glory; when shame and reproach were heaped on him by all hands. When all the disciples had forsaken him, and were fled. Not one left to proclaim his innocence, or speak a word in his vindication. Then does the providence of God as strangely, as powerfully, over-rule the heart and pen of Pilate, to draw this title for him, and affix it to his cross. Surely we must look higher than Pilate in this thing, and see how Providence serves itself by the hands of Christ's adversities. Pilate writes in honour of Christ, and stiffly defends it too. Hence our observation is,

Doct. 1. That the dignity of Christ was openly proclaimed, and defended by an enemy; and that, in the time of his greatest reproaches and sufferings.

To open this mystery of providence to you, that you may not stand idly gazing upon Christ's title, as many then did; we must, First, Consider the nature and quality of this title. Secondly, What hand the Providence of God had in this matter. Thirdly, and then draw forth the proper uses and improvements of it.

First, To open the nature and quality of Christ's title or inscription; let it be thoroughly considered, and we shall find,

First, That it was an extraordinary title, varying from all examples of that kind; and directly crossing the main design and end of their own custom. For, as I hinted before, the end of it was to clear the equity of their proceedings, and show the people how justly they suffered those punishments inflicted on them for such crimes. But lo, here is a title expressing no crime at all, and so vindicating Christ's innocence. This some of them perceived, and moved Pilate to change It, not, This is, but, This is he that said, I am the King of the Jews. In that, as they conceived, lay his crime. O how strange and wonderful a thing was this! But what shall we say! It was a day of wonders and extraordinary things. As there was never such a person crucified before, so there was never such a title affixed to the cross before.

Then does the providence of God as strangely, as powerfully, over-rule the heart and pen of Pilate.

Secondly, As it was an extraordinary, so it was a public title, both written and published with the greatest advantage of spreading itself far and near, among all people, that could be, "for it was written in three languages, and to those most known in the world at that time." The Greek tongue was then known in most parts of the world. The Hebrew was the Jews native language. And the Latin the language of the Romans. So that it being written in Hebrew, Greek, and Latin, it was easy to be understood both by Jews and Gentiles.

And indeed, unto this the providence of God had a special eye, to make it notorious and evident to all the world; for even so all things designed for public view, and knowledge were written. Josephus tells us of certain pillars, on which was engraven in letters of Greek, and Latin, "It is a wickedness for strangers to enter into the holy place". So the soldiers of Gordian, the third emperor, when he was slain upon the borders of Persia, raised a monument for him, and engraved his memorial upon it, in Greek, Latin, Persia, Judaic, and Egyptian letters, that all people might read the same. And as it was written in three learned languages, so it was exposed to view in a public place; and at that time, when multitudes of strangers, as well as Jews, were at Jerusalem; it was at the time of the passover; so that all things concurred to spread and divulge the innocence of Christ, vindicated in this title.

Thirdly, As it was a public, so it was an honourable title. Such was the nature of it, saith Bucer; that in the midst of death, Christ began to triumph by it. And by reason thereof, the cross began to change its own nature, and instead of a rack, or engine of torture, it became a throne of majesty. Yea, it might be called now, as the church itself is, The pillar and ground of truth; for it held out much of the gospel, much of the glory of Christ; as that pillar does, to which a royal proclamation is affixed.

Fourthly, It was a vindicating title: it cleared up the honour, dignity, and innocence of Christ, against all the false imputations, calumnies, and blasphemies, which are cast upon him before, by the wicked tongues, both of Jews and Gentiles.

They had called him a deceiver, and usurper, a blasphemer; they rent their clothes, in token of their detestation of his blasphemy; because he made himself the Son of God, and King of Israel. But now in this, they acknowledged him to be both Lord and Saviour. Not a mock king, as they had made him before. So that herein the honour of Christ was fully vindicated.

All things concurred to spread and divulge the innocence of Christ.

Fifthly, Moreover it was a predicting and presaging title. Evidently foreshowing the propagation of Christ's kingdom, and the spreading of his name and glory among all kindreds, nations, tongues, and languages. As Christ has right to enter into all the kingdoms of the earth, by his gospel, and set up his throne in every nation: so it was presaged by this title that he should do so. And that both Hebrews, Greeks, and Latins should be called to the knowledge of him. Nor is it a wonder, that this should be predicted by wicked Pilate, when Caiaphas himself, a man every way as wicked as he, had prophesied to the same purpose, John 11:51, 52. For being High-Priest that year, he prophesied, That Jesus should die for that nation, and not for that nation only, but that also he should gather together in one, the children of God that were scattered abroad. Yea, many have prophesied in Christ's name, who, for all that, shall never be owned by him, Matth. 7:22.

Sixthly, And lastly, It was an immutable title. The Jews endeavoured, but could not persuade Pilate to alter it. To all their importunities he returns this resolute answer, "What I have written, I have written," as if he should say, Urge me no more, I have written his title, I cannot, I will not, alter a letter, a point thereof. "Surely the constancy of Pilate at this time can be attributed to nothing but divine special Providence." Most wonderful! that he, who before was as inconstant as a reed shaken by the wind, is now as fixed as a pillar of brass.

Pilate was a wicked man, and had no love to Christ.

And yet more wonderful, that he should write down that very particular in the title of Christ, This is the King of the Jews, which was the very thing that so scared him but a little before, and was the very consideration that moved him to give sentence. What was now become of the fear of Caesar? That Pilate dares to be Christ's herald, and publicly to proclaim him, a King of the Jews. This was the title.

Secondly, We shall next enquire what hand the Divine Providence had in this business.

And indeed, the providence of God in this hour, acted gloriously, and wonderfully, these five ways.

First, In over-ruling the heart and hand of Pilate in the draught and stile of it, and that contrary to his own inclination. I doubt not but Pilate himself was ignorant of, and far enough from designing that which the wisdom of providence aimed at in this matter. He was a wicked man, and had no love to Christ. He had given sentence of death against him; yet this is he that proclaimed him to be Jesus, King of the Jews. It so over-ruled his pen, that he could not write what was in his own heart and intention, but the quite contrary; even a fair and public testimony of the kingly office of the Son of God, This is the King of the Jews.

Secondly, Herein the wisdom of Providence was gloriously displayed, in applying a present, proper, public remedy to the reproaches and blasphemies which Christ had then newly received in his name and honour. The superstitious Jews wound him, and Heathen Pilate prepares a plaister to heal him: they reproach, he vindicates; they throw the dirt, he washes it off. Oh the profound and inscrutable wisdom of Providence!

Thirdly, Moreover, Providence eminently appeared at this time in keeping so timorous a person, a man of so base a spirit, that would not

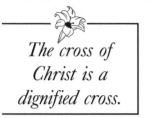

The cross of Christ is a dignified cross.

stick at any thing to please the people, from receding, or giving ground in the least to their importunities. Is Pilate become a man of such resolution and constancy? Whence is this? But from the God of the spirits of all flesh, who now flowed in so powerfully upon his spirit, that he could not choose but write; and when he had written, had no more power to alter what he had written, than he had to refuse to write it.

Fourthly, Herein also much of the wisdom of Providence appeared, in casting the ignominy of the death of Christ upon those very men who ought to bear it. Pilate was moved by divine instinct, at once to clear Christ, and accuse them. For it is as if he had said, you have moved me to crucify your king, I have crucified him, and now let the ignominy of his death rest upon your heads, who have extorted this from me. He is righteous, the crime is not his but yours.

Fifthly, And lastly, The providence of God wonderfully discovered itself (as before was noted) in fixing this title to the cross of Christ, when there was so great a confluence of all sorts of people to take notice of it. So that it could never have been more advantageously published, than it was at this time. So that we may say, How wonderful are the works of God! "His ways are in the sea, his paths in the great deeps; his footsteps are not known." His providence has a prospect beyond the understandings of all creatures.

Did Pilate affix such an honourable, vindicating title to the cross? Then the cross of Christ is a dignified cross. Then the cross and sufferings of Christ are attended with glory and honour. Remember when your hearts begin to startle at the sufferings and reproaches of Christ, there is an honourable title upon the cross of Christ. And as it was upon his, so it will be upon your cross also, if ye suffer for Christ.

—JOHN FLAVEL
From *The Fountain of Life*

One Crown Not Any Seek

One crown not any seek,
And yet the highest head
Its isolation coveted,
Its stigma deified.

While Pontius Pilate lives,
In whatsoever hell,
That coronation pierces him.
He recollects it well.

—EMILY DICKINSON

EMILY DICKINSON (1830–1886)—Emily Dickinson was born in Amherst, Massachusetts on December 10, 1830. She lived the majority of her life alone in her house, except for attending Amherst Academy and Holyoke Female Seminary for a short time. She was reportedly a very social and energetic girl, but in her mid-twenties, she became very reclusive. Her loneliness is evident in her poems, but they are also extremely inspirational. Dickinson wrote hundreds of poems and often included them in letters to friends, but it wasn't until after her death in 1886 that her poems were discovered and she became widely recognized. It is estimated that she wrote over 1,700 poems. The first volume of her work wasn't published until 1890.

John 19

Here are some remarkable circumstances of Christ's dying more fully related than before, which those will take special notice of who covet to know Christ and him crucified. The title set up over his head. Observe, 1. The inscription itself which Pilate wrote, and ordered to be fixed to the top of the cross, declaring the cause for which he was crucified, v. 19. Matthew called it, *aitia—the accusation;* Mark and Luke called it *epigraphe—*

the inscription; John calls it by the proper Latin name, *titlos—the title:* and it was this, *Jesus of Nazareth, the King of the Jews,* Pilate intended this for his reproach, that he, being *Jesus of Nazareth,* should pretend to be king of the Jews, and set up in competition with Caesar, to whom Pilate would thus recommend himself, as very jealous for his honour and interest, when he would treat but a titular king, a king in metaphor, as the worst of malefactors; but God overruled this matter, (1.) That it might be a further testimony to the innocency of our Lord Jesus; for here was an accusation which, as it was worded, contained no crime. If this be all they have to lay to his charge,

> *This is Jesus,*
> *a Saviour,*
> *sanctified*
> *to God.*

surely he has done nothing worthy of death or of bonds. (2.) That it might show forth his dignity and honour. This is Jesus a Saviour, *Nazoraios,* the blessed Nazarite, sanctified to God; this is the *king of the Jews, Messiah the prince,* the *sceptre* that *should rise out of Israel,* as Balaam had foretold; dying for the good of his people, as Caiaphas had foretold. Thus all these three bad men witnessed to Christ, though they meant not so. 2. The notice taken of this inscription (v. 20): *Many of the Jews read it,* not only those of Jerusalem, but those out of the country, and from other countries, strangers and proselytes, that came up to worship at the feast. Multitudes read it, and it occasioned a great variety of reflections and speculations, as men stood affected. Christ himself was set for a sign, a title. Here are two reasons why the title was so much read: (1.) Because the place where Jesus was crucified, though without the gate, was yet *nigh the city,* which intimates that if it had been any great distance off they would not have been led, no not by their curiosity, to go and see it, and read it. It is an advantage to have the means of knowing Christ brought to our doors. (2.) Because it was written in Hebrew, and Greek, and Latin, which made it legible by all; they all understood one or other of these languages, and none were more careful to bring up their children to read than the Jews generally were. It likewise made it the more considerable; everyone would be curious to enquire what it was which was so industriously published in the three most known languages. In the Hebrew the oracles of God were recorded; in Greek the learning of the philosophers; and in Latin the laws of the empire. In each of these Christ is proclaimed king, in whom are hid all the treasures of revelation, wisdom, and power. God so ordering it that this should be written in the three then most known tongues, it was intimated thereby that Jesus Christ should be a Saviour to all nations, and not to the Jews only; and also that every nation should hear *in their own tongue the wonderful works* of the Redeemer. Hebrew, Greek, and Latin, were the vulgar languages at that time in this part of the world; so that this is so far from intimating (as the Papists would have it) that the scripture is still to be retained in these three languages, that on the contrary it teaches us that the knowledge of Christ ought to be diffused throughout every nation in their own tongue, as the proper vehicle of it, that people may converse as freely with the scriptures as they do with their neighbours. (3.) The offence which the prosecutors took at it, v. 21. They would not have it written, *the king of the Jews;* but that he said of himself, *I am the king of the Jews.* Here they show themselves, (1.) Very spiteful and malicious against Christ. It was not enough to have him crucified, but they must have his name crucified too. To justify themselves in giving him such bad treatment, they thought themselves concerned to give him a bad character, and to represent him as a usurper of honours and powers that he was not entitled to. (2.) Foolishly jealous of the honour of their nation. Though they were a conquered and enslaved people, yet they stood so much upon the punctilio of their reputation that they scorned to have it said that this was their king. (3.) Very impertinent and troublesome to Pilate. They could not but be sensible that they had forced him, against his mind, to condemn Christ, and yet, in such a trivial thing as this, they continue to tease him; and it was so much the worse in that, though they had charged him with pretending to be the king of the Jews, yet they had not proved it, nor had he ever said so. 4. The judge's resolution to adhere to it: "*What I have written I have written,* and will not alter it to humour them." (1.) Hereby an affront was put upon the chief priests, who would still be dictating. It seems, by Pilate's manner of speaking, that he was uneasy in himself for yielding to them, and vexed at them for forcing him to it, and therefore he was resolved to be cross with them; and by this inscription he insinuates, [1.] That, notwithstanding their pretences, they were not sincere in their affections to Caesar and his government; they were willing enough to have a king of the Jews, if they could have one to their mind. [2.] That such a king as this, so mean and despicable, was good enough to be the king of the Jews; and this would be the fate of all that should dare to oppose the Roman power. [3.] That they had been very unjust and unreasonable in prosecuting this Jesus, when there was no fault to be found in him. (2.) Hereby honour was done to the Lord Jesus. Pilate stuck to it with resolution, that he was the king of the Jews. What he had written was what God had first written, and therefore he could not alter it; for thus it was written, that Messiah the prince should be *cut off,* Dan. 9:26. This therefore is the true cause of his death; he dies because the king of Israel must die, must thus die. When the Jews reject Christ, and will not have him for their king, Pilate, a Gentile, sticks to it that he is a king, which was an earnest of what came to pass soon after, when the Gentiles submitted to the kingdom of the Messiah, which the unbelieving Jews had rebelled against.

—MATTHEW HENRY
From *Commentary on the Whole Bible*

> **MATTHEW HENRY** (1662–1714)—Matthew Henry is best known for his devotional commentary on the Bible. He was also a distinguished preacher at age 24, and was a pastor at various churches until his death. His preaching was popular for its scriptural content, lucid presentation, practical application, and Christ-centeredness.

And Joseph and His Mother Marveled

Et erat ejus et mirantes super his quae dicebantur de illo.

("And Joseph and his mother marveled at those things which were spoken of him.")

—LUKE 2:33

Our Lord Jesus Christ, my brethren, is a hero, a hero all the world wants. You know how books of tales are written, that put one man before the reader and shew him off handsome for the most part and brave and call him My Hero or Our Hero. Often mothers make a hero of a son; girls of a sweetheart and good wives of a husband. Soldiers make a hero of a great general, a party of its leader, a nation of any great man that brings it glory, whether king, warrior statesman, thinker, poet, or whatever it shall be. But Christ, he is the hero. He too is the hero of a book or books, of the divine Gospels. He is a warrior and a conqueror; of whom it is written he went forth conquering and to conquer. He is a king, Jesus of Nazareth king of the Jews, though when he came to his own kingdom his own did not receive him, and now, his people having cast him off, we Gentiles are his inheritance. He is a statesman, that drew up the New Testament in his blood and founded the Roman Catholic Church that cannot fail. He is a thinker, that taught us divine mysteries. He is an orator and poet, as in his eloquent words and parables appears. He is all the world's hero, the desire of

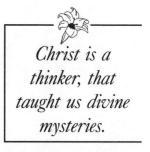

Christ is a thinker, that taught us divine mysteries.

nations. But besides he is the hero of single souls; his mother's hero, not out of motherly foolish fondness but because he was, as the angel told her, great and the son of the Most High and all that he did and said was done and said about him she laid up in her heart. He is the true-love and the bridegroom of men's souls: the virgins follow him whithersoever he goes; the martyrs follow him through a sea of blood, through great tribulation; all his servants take up their cross and follow him, own him a hero, and wish they dared answer to his call.

—GERARD MANLEY HOPKINS
From *Tongues of Angels, Tongues of Men*

Telling the Truth: The Gospel as Tragedy, Comedy, and Fairy Tale
(Excerpt)

The secretary lowers her eyes under his steady, bland gaze like a girl in a convent, but he has reason to know that if there was ever a convent, she has come a long way since and wouldn't need more than a nod from him to come a good bit farther still. He is tempted for a moment to give her that nod but is deterred by his knowledge that a man needs as much singleness of purpose to be unfaithful to his wife as he needs to be faithful to her, and for the moment the only purpose he can bring himself to take seriously is lunch, which he eats quickly and alone at his desk. Roman beer, cold chicken with mayonnaise, two hard-boiled eggs, and if smoking doesn't get him, he thinks, cholesterol will. He is already older than his father lived to be, and bad hearts run in the family. When he is through eating, he would trade the Ostian villa for a cigarette, but cigarettes are death, and he has flushed them all away for the sake of life. It is a sacrifice, he hopes, that will prove worth the making.

The up-country messiah stands in front of Pilate's desk with his hands tied behind his back.

A phone call comes through from his wife. She tells him that one of the horses has gotten foundered and has to be put down. She doesn't give a hoot about horses, but as she runs on and on about it, all of a sudden her voice goes queer and thick, and he realizes that she is weeping. He can see her sitting there with the receiver cradled between her ear and her shoulder so that she can light a cigarette as she always does when she starts to cry. He can almost smell the smoke as she lights it and then starts talking again. He closes his eyes and tries to think of something to distract her with, but nothing comes.

She is apologizing for bothering him, for weeping, apologizing for her life. She has had a bad night, the same dark dreams . . . As she talks, he swivels around in his chair to look out the window behind him. Down in the courtyard a ragged child is talking to one of the soldiers, and he wonders if it can be one of the epidemic children, the disease clinging to its clothes like lice. A pigeon perched on the windowsill fans one wing out, then tucks it in again. When his wife finally hangs up and he swings back to his desk, he finds he is no longer alone. They have brought the up-country messiah in for questioning. Pilate is caught off-guard, and before he knows what he is doing, he takes a cigarette from an onyx box on his desk and lights it.

The man stands in front of the desk with his hands tied behind his back. You can see that he has been roughed up a little. His upper lip is absurdly puffed out and one eye is swollen shut. He looks unwashed and smells unwashed. His feet are bare—big, flat peasant feet although the man himself is not big. There is something almost comic about the way he stands there, bent slightly forward because of the way his hands are tied and goggling down at the floor through his one good eye as if he is looking for something he has lost, a button off his shirt or a dime somebody slipped him for a cup of coffee. If there were just the two of them, Pilate thinks, he would give him his carfare and send him back to the sticks where he came from, but the guards are still watching, and on the wall the official portrait of Tiberius Caesar is watching, the fat, powdered face, the toothy imperial smile, so he goes through the formalities.

"So you're the king of the Jews," *Pilate says.*

"So you're the king of the Jews," he says. "The head Jew," because there hasn't been one of them yet who hasn't made that his claim—David came back to give Judea back to the Jews.

The man says, "It's not this world I'm king of," but his accent is so thick that Pilate hardly gets it, the accent together with what they have done to his upper lip. As if he has a mouth full of stones, he says, "I've come to bear witness to the truth," and at that the procurator of Judea takes such a deep drag on his filter tip that his head swims and for a moment he's afraid he may faint.

He pushes back from the desk and crosses his legs. There is the papery rustle of wings as the pigeon flutters off the sill and floats down toward the cobbles. Standing by the door, the guards aren't paying much attention. One of them is picking his nose, the other staring up at the ceiling. Cigarette smoke drifts over the surface of the desk—the picture of his wife when she still had her looks, the onyx box from Caesar, the clay plaque with the imprint of his son's hand on it, made while he was still a child in nursery school. Pilate squints at the man through the smoke and asks his questions.

He asks it half because he would give as much as even his life to hear the answer and half because he believes there is no answer and would give a good deal to hear that too because it would mean just one thing less to have to worry about. He says, "What is truth?" and by way of an answer, the man with the split lip doesn't say a blessed thing. You could hear a pin drop in the big, high-ceilinged room with Tiberius grinning down from the wall like a pumpkin, that one cigarette a little unsteady between the procurator's yellowed fingertips.

> *The one who hears the truth that is silence before it is a word is Pilate, and he hears it because he has asked to hear it, and he has asked to hear it.*

The one who hears the truth that is silence before it is a word is Pilate, and he hears it because he has asked to hear it, and he has asked to hear it—"What is truth?" he asks—because in a world of many truths and half truths, he is hungry for truth itself or, failing that, at least for the truth that there is no truth. We are all of us Pilate in our asking after truth, and when we come to church to ask it, the preacher would do well to answer us also with silence because the truth and the Gospel are one, and before the Gospel is a word, it too like truth is silence— not an ordinary silence, silence as nothing to hear, but silence that makes itself heard if you listen to it the way Pilate listens to the silence of the man with the split lip. The Gospel that is truth is good news, but before it is good news, let us say that it is just news. Let us say that it is evening news, the television news, but with the sound turned off.

—FREDERICH BUECHNER

FREDERICH BUECHNER—Frederich Buechner is one of the most prolific writers of our modern era. An author on many subjects, Buechner has defined the subject of forgiveness in this way: "To forgive somebody is to say one way or another, 'You have done something unspeakable, and by all rights I should call it quits between us. Both my pride and my principles demand no less. However, although I make no guarantees that I will be able to forget what you've done and though we may both carry the scars for life, I refuse to let it stand between us. I still want you to be my friend.'"

A Violent Grace
(Excerpt)

The soldiers were assigned the task of executing Jesus.

These men were almost certainly mercenaries—killers for hire—in the Roman army. Gentiles from various parts of the empire, they would have had only a nodding acquaintance with Jewish customs. For them, Jews were a mysterious and unpredictable lot, and a crucifixion was just another day's work.

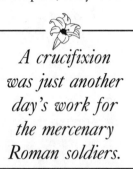

A crucifixion was just another day's work for the mercenary Roman soldiers.

Compared to other forms of execution, a crucifixion at least gave them the pleasure of tormenting their victims. They took delight in nailing the written charge against Christ on the titulus above His head: "King of the Jews."

"If you are the King of the Jews," they shouted as Jesus writhed on the cross, "save yourself!" They defied Him to unfasten even one nail.

Their "if" reminds me of Satan's temptation of Jesus in the wilderness: "If you are the Son of God . . ." And again, even though Jesus was both King and Son, He refused to prove it. Instead, He humbled Himself and became, in Paul's words, "obedient to death—even death on a cross" (Philippians 2:8).

—MICHAEL CARD

John 19:19–22

19. *And Pilate wrote also a title.* The Evangelist relates a memorable action of Pilate, after having pronounced the sentence. It is perhaps true that it was customary to affix *titles,* when malefactors were executed, that the cause of the punishment might be known to all, and might

serve the purpose of an example. But in Christ there is this extraordinary circumstance, that the *title* which is affixed to him implies no disgrace; for Pilate's intention was, to avenge himself indirectly on the Jews, (who, by their obstinacy, had extorted from him an unjust sentence of death on an innocent man) and, in the person of Christ, to throw blame on the whole nation. Thus he does not brand Christ with the commission of any crime.

> *It did not, indeed, occur to Pilate to celebrate Christ as the Author of salvation.*

But the providence of God, which guided the pen of Pilate, had a higher object in view. It did not, indeed, occur to Pilate to celebrate Christ as the Author of salvation, and the Nazarene of *God,* and the King of a chosen people; but God dictated to him this commendation of the Gospel, though he knew not the meaning of what he wrote. It was the same secret guidance of the Spirit that caused *the title* to be published in three languages; for it is not probable that this was an ordinary practice, but the Lord showed, by this preparatory arrangement, that the time was now at hand, when the name of his Son should be made known throughout the whole earth.

21. *The chief priests of the Jews said therefore to Pilate.* They feel that they are sharply rebuked; and, therefore, they would wish that *the title* were changed, so as not to involve the nation in disgrace, but to throw the whole blame on Christ. But yet they do not conceal their deep hatred of the truth, since the smallest spark of it is more than they are able to endure. Thus Satan always prompts his servants to endeavor to extinguish, or, at least, to choke, by their own darkness, the light of God, as soon as the feeblest ray of it appears.

22. *What I have written I have written.* Pilate's firmness must be ascribed to the providence of God; for there can be no doubt that they attempted, in various ways, to change his resolution. Let us know, therefore, that he was held by a Divine hand, so that he remained unmoved. Pilate did not yield to the prayers of the priests, and did not allow himself to be corrupted by them; but God testified, by his mouth, the firmness and stability of the kingdom of his Son. And if, in the writing of Pilate, the

kingdom of Christ was shown to be so firm that it could not be shaken by all the attacks of its enemies, what value ought we to attach to the testimonies of the Prophets, whose tongues and hands God consecrated to his service?

The example of *Pilate* reminds us, also, that it is our duty to remain steady in defending the truth. A heathen refuses to retract what he has justly and properly written concerning Christ, though he did not understand or consider what he was doing. How great, then, will be our dishonor, if, terrified by threatenings or dangers, we withdraw from the profession of his doctrine, which God hath sealed on our hearts by his Spirit! Besides, it ought to be observed how detestable is the tyranny of the Papists, which prohibits the reading of the Gospel, and of the whole of the Scripture, by the common people. Pilate, though he was a reprobate man, and, in other respects,

It is our duty to remain steady in defending the truth.

an instrument of Satan, was nevertheless, by a secret guidance, appointed to be a herald of the Gospel, that he might publish a short summary of it in three languages. What rank, therefore, shall we assign to those who do all that they can to suppress the knowledge of it, since they show that they are worse than Pilate?

—JOHN CALVIN
From *Commentary on the Gospel According to John*

JOHN CALVIN (1509–1564)—Best known for his works on theology, John Calvin was one of the most important figures in the Reformation. In 1533, he delivered a speech calling for reforms in the established church. The result was not change, but it incited a wave of anti-Protestant sentiment that eventually threatened his life and caused him to flee. He was then convinced to stay in Geneva and work among the Protestants there. In 1541, pro-Protestant forces gained control of the city and Geneva became a refuge for Protestants all over Europe. Calvin's famed theology consists of the belief in the primacy of the scripture as an authority for doctrinal decisions, a belief in predestination, and a belief in salvation wholly accomplished by grace with no influence from works.

Foxe's Book of Martyrs
(Excerpt)

The faithful, while they were dragged along, proceeded with cheerful steps; their countenances shone with much grace and glory; their bonds were as the most beautiful ornaments; and they themselves looked as brides adorned with their richest array, breathing the fragrance of Christ. They were put to death in various ways: or, in other words, they wove a chaplet of various odours and flowers, and presented it to the Father.

Maturus, Sanctus, Blandina, and Attalus, were led to the wild beasts into the amphitheatre to be the common spectacle of Gentile inhumanity.

Attalus also was vehemently demanded by the multitude, for he was a person of great reputation among us. He advanced in all the cheerfulness and serenity of a good conscience;—an experienced Christian, and ever ready and active in bearing testimony to the truth. He was led round the amphitheatre, and a tablet carried before him, inscribed "This is Attalus the Christian." The rage of the people would have had him dispatched immediately; but the governor, understanding that he was a Roman, ordered him back to prison: and concerning him and others, who could plead the same privilege of Roman citizenship, he wrote to the emperor and waited for his instructions. Caesar sent orders that the confessors of Christ should be put to death. Roman citizens had the privilege of dying by decollation; the rest were exposed to wild beasts.

The One People Once Called

The one people once called
King in jest, God in fact,
Who was killed, and whose implement of torture

Was heated by the warmth of my breast . . .
The disciples of Christ tasted death,
And the old gossips, and the soldiers,
And the procurator from Rome—all gone.
There, where once the arch rose,
Where the sea splashed, where the cliff turned black,
They were imbibed with wine, inhaled with the stifling dust
And the fragrance of immortal roses.
Gold rusts and steel decays,
Marble crumbles away. Everything is on the verge of death.
The most reliable thing on earth is sorrow,
And the most enduring—the almighty Word.

> —ANNA AKHMATOVA
> From *Divine Inspiration: The*
> *Life of Jesus in World Poetry*

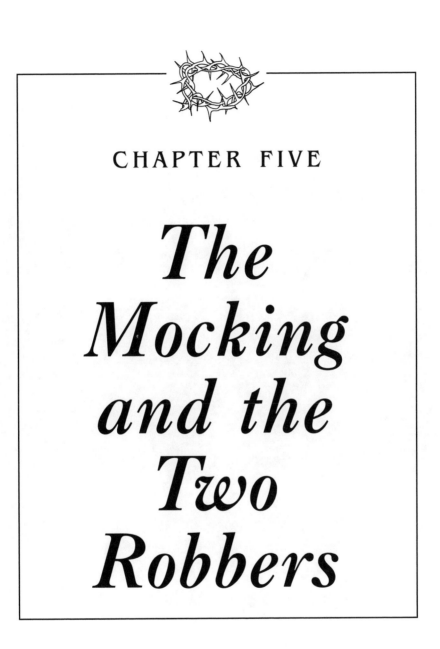

CHAPTER FIVE

The Mocking and the Two Robbers

The Mocking and
the Two Robbers

MATTHEW 27:38–44

³⁸*Then two robbers were crucified with Him, one on the right and another on the left.* ³⁹*And those who passed by blasphemed Him, wagging their heads* ⁴⁰*and saying, "You who destroy the temple and build it in three days, save Yourself! If You are the Son of God, come down from the cross."* ⁴¹*Likewise the chief priests also, mocking with the scribes and elders, said,* ⁴²*"He saved others; Himself He cannot save. If He is the King of Israel, let Him now come down from the cross, and we will believe Him.* ⁴³*He trusted in God; let Him deliver Him now if He will have Him; for He said, 'I am the Son of God.'"* ⁴⁴*Even the robbers who were crucified with Him reviled Him with the same thing.*

LUKE 23:32–43

³²*There were also two others, criminals, led with Him to be put to death.* ³³*And when they had come to the place called Calvary, there they crucified Him, and the criminals, one on the right hand and the other on the left. . . .* ³⁵*And the people stood looking on. But even the rulers with them sneered, saying, "He saved others; let Him save Himself if He is the Christ, the chosen of God."* ³⁶*The soldiers also mocked Him, coming and offering Him sour wine,* ³⁷*and saying, "If You are the King of the Jews, save Yourself." . . .* ³⁹*Then one of the criminals who were hanged blasphemed Him, saying, "If You are the Christ, save Yourself and us."* ⁴⁰*But the other, answering, rebuked him, saying, "Do you not even fear God, seeing you are under the same condemnation?* ⁴¹*And we indeed justly, for we receive the due reward of our deeds; but this Man has done nothing wrong."* ⁴²*Then he said to Jesus, "Lord, remember me when You come into Your kingdom."* ⁴³*And Jesus said to him, "Assuredly, I say to you, today you will be with Me in Paradise."*

Luke XXIII

Gentile or Hebrew or simply a man
Whose face has been lost in time;
We shall not ransom from oblivion
The silent letters of his name.

He knows of clemency what could
Be known by a petty thief Judea had
Nailed to a cross. Of the preceding time,
We can, today, find nothing. In his final

Task of death by crucifixion,
He heard, among the taunts of the crowd,
That the one who was dying next to him
Was God, and he said, blindly:

Remember me when you come into
Your kingdom, and the inconceivable voice
That will one day be judge of every being
Promised, from the terrible cross,

Paradise. They said nothing more Until
   the end, but history
Will not allow the memory to die
Of that afternoon in which these two died.

Oh friends, the innocence of this friend
Of Jesus Christ, the candor that made him

Ask for and be granted Paradise
From the ignominy of punishment

Was what tossed him many times
To son, to the blood-stained gamble.

    —JORGE LUIS BORGES, translated
    from the Spanish by David Curzon
    From *The Gospels in Our Image*

The Life of Christ
(Excerpt)

The members of the Sanhedrin then joined in taunting Him. "He saved others," they said, "Himself He cannot save. If He be the King of Israel, let Him now come down from the cross, and we will believe Him. He trusted in God; let Him now deliver Him, if He will have Him; for He said: I am the Son of God."

There is something peculiarly offensive in deriding anyone in the third person while that person is within earshot, and the atheistic priests and gloating ancients used that form to assail Christ's Divinity. But their very mockery was a profession of belief in His miracles, in those "works" to which time and again He had pointed as proof of His divine power; for they said: "He saved others." They avowed that they would believe in Him if He came down from the cross; although, as a matter of fact, the majority of them refused to believe in Him even after He arose from the dead. Mockery and sarcasm are not the usual preparations for an act of faith.

> *The members of the Sanhedrin avowed that they would believe in Him if He came down from the cross.*

The soldiers caught the spirit of the crowd; arising, they stood around the cross, and lifting their drinking cups, offered Jesus a drink and toast: "If Thou be the King of the Jews," they taunted, "save Thyself."

All these jeering challenges gave an idea to the robber hanging at His left. Being a Jew, he knew something of the Messiah, and this knowledge he revealed in his request: "If Thou be Christ, save Thyself and us."

His words included his companion, hanging on the other side of Christ; but the second thief refused to be thus represented. He spoke for himself.

> *Jesus said, "Amen I say to thee, this day thou shalt be with Me in paradise."*

His was in an entirely different cast of mind from that of the first thief. It was capable for deep penetration; and criminal though he was, there was something generous in his nature. Christ's appearance and attitude told him plainly that He was innocent.

"Neither dost thou fear God," he asked his accomplice, "seeing thou art under the same condemnation?" That is, he was about to die; and instead of mocking a fellow-sufferer, he should have been preparing for his own judgment. The law was punishing both for actual crimes, and that, "indeed justly," as he reminded the first thief, "for we receive the due reward of our deeds; but this Man hath done no evil." Then turning to Jesus he said: "Lord, remember me when Thou shalt come into Thy kingdom." His was a perfect act of faith, and Jesus answered it with His Second Word from the cross: "Amen I say to thee, this day thou shalt be with Me in paradise."

Both malefactors had asked a favor of Jesus, the first with a taunt for temporal relief, the second with a prayer for eternal salvation. He granted the second.

—ISIDORE O'BRIEN

Calvary

Friendless and faint, with martyred steps and slow,
Faint for the flesh, but for the spirit free,
Stung by the mob that came to see the show,
The Master toiled along to Calvary;

We gibed him, as he went, with houndish glee
Till his dimmed eyes for us did overflow;
We cursed his vengeless hands thrice wretchedly,—
And this was nineteen hundred years ago.

But after nineteen hundred years the shame
Still clings, and we have not made good the loss
That outraged faith has entered in his name.
Ah, when shall come love's courage to be strong!
Tell me, O Lord—tell me, O Lord, how long
Are we to keep Christ writhing on the cross!

—EDWIN ARLINGTON ROBINSON
From *The Gospels in Our Image*

Upon a Hill

Three men shared death upon a hill,
But only one man died;
The other two—
A thief and God himself—
Made rendezvous.

Three crosses still
Are borne up Calvary's Hill,
Where Sin lifts them high:
Upon the one sag broken man
Who, cursing, die;

Another holds the praying thief,
Or those who, penitent as he,
Still find the Christ
Beside them on the tree.

—MIRIAM LEFEVRE CROUSE
From *Christ in Poetry*

Judge Not

The first one home is a thief. Jesus is not very fastidious about the company he keeps. A serious question is raised about whether we will be happy with those who are with us in paradise—assuming, for the moment, that we will be there. That question comes later.

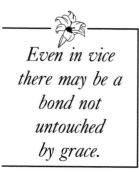

Even in vice there may be a bond not untouched by grace.

Recall now the two criminals. Mentioned in all four Gospels, they were called thieves by two of the Gospel writers. Whatever else they had stolen in their lives, the one, commonly called "the good thief," stole at the end of a reward he did not deserve. There they were, hoisted on their crosses, one to the left of Jesus, the other on the right, much as Matthew 25 depicts the final judgment of humanity with the goats on the left and the sheep on the right. The good thief is a found sheep. More accurately, he is a goat who was made an honorary sheep just before his time ran out.

Both thieves may have heard about Jesus before. If not, they certainly heard about him that day, hanging there on their crosses and surrounded by the mocking crowds. The one thief joined in the mockery with cutting scorn borne of his own desperate plight. "Are you not the Christ? Save Yourself and us!" Luke tells us that he "railed" against Jesus. Note that there was perhaps a touch of goodness in the man. He did not say, "Save yourself and me," but, "Save yourself and us." Maybe the other thief was a friend; maybe they were partners in crime. Even in vice there may be a bond not untouched by grace. But whatever grace was there was crushed by the anger and contempt with which he turned against Jesus, the source of grace. In his dying he turned, and it seems he turned definitively, against the light.

Not so with the other one. The other thief rebuked the first, we are told. "Do you not fear God, since you are under the same sentence of condemnation? And we indeed justly; for we are receiving the due reward of our deeds; but this man has done nothing wrong." Painfully twisting his neck, he looked toward Jesus. "Jesus," he said, "remember me when you come into your kingdom." And Jesus said to him, "Truly, I say to you, today you will be with me in paradise." In his dying, the second thief turned toward the light.

Note that this is the only time in any Gospel account that someone addresses Jesus simply by name. Otherwise it is always "Jesus Son of God," "Jesus Son of David" or some other form of particular respect. The first person to be so familiar is a convicted criminal who is the last person to speak to Jesus before he dies. Dying together is a great social leveler. The Greek text suggests that this was a persistent plea, that he "was speaking" to Jesus. But maybe it wasn't really a plea at all. Maybe he was trying to comfort Jesus.

In her play *The Man Born to Be King*, Dorothy Sayers portrays the good thief—Dysmas as legend calls him—as taking pity on Jesus.

According to Sayers, Dysmas turned toward the light, but he did not believe in the light. His "Lord, remember me" was not an act of faith but an act of charity. It is the kind of thing one might say to someone who imagines he is Napoleon. But then, says Sayers, with Jesus' unexpected answer there is a moment of illumination, of insight; it is not unlike an act of faith. Of Dysmas she writes: "He is confused between the crucified man, of whose weakness it would be selfish to demand one added agony, and the eternal Christ, of whose strength he is half-aware, and with whose sufferings he seems to be mysteriously identified, so that in some strange way each is bearing the pain of the other."

> *Jesus was bearing the pain of the thieves, and of all humanity half aware and unaware.*

Certainly Jesus was bearing the pain of Dysmas, and of the other thief, and of all humanity half aware and unaware. "Today you will be with me in paradise." Jesus does not reject any who turn to him. At times we turn to him with little faith, at times with a mix of faith and doubt when we are more sure of the doubt than of the faith. Jesus is not fastidious about the quality of faith. He takes what he can get, so to speak, and gives immeasurably more than he receives. He takes our faith more seriously than we do and makes of it more than we ever could. His response to our faith is greater than our faith.

—RICHARD JOHN NEUHAUS
From *Death on a Friday Afternoon*

RICHARD JOHN NEUHAUS—Richard John Neuhaus was one of eight children and the son of a Lutheran Pastor. He followed his father into ministry and spent 30 years as a Lutheran pastor in a poor community in Brooklyn, New York. He was a well-known public commentator and the founder and director of the Centre for Religion and Society in New York. His conversion to Catholicism in 1990 stunned members of the Lutheran Church. He is the author of *The Naked Public Square* and *The Catholic Movement*.

The Suffering God

The cross they raised against the rain
  Of hideous boasts and cruel jeers
Bent down one head in human pain
  And lifted two old fears.

The one, a death that marked defeat,
  Laid darkness on the crying earth.
But in that darkness God could meet
  With men in their rebirth.

The other moved beneath the cross,
  A hidden fear that God might keep
Himself aloof—a visioned loss,
  That God could never weep.

Now darkness is dispelled with light
   Flaming the cross and the dark sky,
For God has suffered through this night
   And taught men how to die.

            —RAYMOND KRESENSKY
            From *Christ in Poetry*

Jesus, Thou Art the Sinner's Friend

Jesus, Thou art the sinner's Friend;
As such I look to Thee;
Now, in the fullness of Thy love,
O Lord, remember me.

Remember Thy pure Word of grace,
Remember Calvary's tree,
Remember all Thy dying groans,
And then remember me.

Thou wondrous Advocate with God,
I yield my soul to Thee;
While Thou art pleading on the throne,
Dear Lord, remember me.

Lord, I am guilty, I am vile,
But Thy salvation's free;
Then, in Thine all abounding grace,
Dear Lord, remember me.

Howe'er forsaken or despised,
Howe'er oppressed I be,
Howe'er forgotten here on earth,
Do Thou remember me.

And when I close my eyes in death,
And human help shall flee,
Then, then, my dear redeeming God,
O then remember me.

—RICHARD BURNHAM

Hope for All Humanity

Tradition has indicated that the three crosses on Calvary formed a semicircle. Jesus of Nazareth hung in the center; the two thieves were at his right and left, yet far enough in front of him so they were able to gaze at each other and at him. It was a clever strategy to torture the victims by allowing them to see in others the degradation to which they themselves had been brought.

As the moments passed, the silence which had fallen over the onlookers while the act of crucifixion was being carried out gave way to taunts. The chief priests pushed their way to the front ranks. Their words tell us that, even with the Galilean hanging on the cross, they were not certain that they had disposed of him. "This fellow saved others," they shouted to the crowd: "Let him save himself if he is God's anointed, the chosen one."

Encouraged by the ridicule heaped upon Jesus by the high officials, the soldiers "made sport of him." One of them offered him sour wine. "Are you the king of the Jews?" he cried. "Save yourself then!"

Jesus did not answer. At that moment the focus of attention shifted from the central cross to those who were hanging with him.

Two thieves! Little is known of their background or offences, save only this: one victim admitted they were guilty of the crimes which had led to their conviction. "We are indeed suffering justly," he said, "for we are receiving due requital for what we have done." We do not know whether they were Galileans, Judeans, Samaritans, or from one of the far provinces. They had been caught in crimes which were punishable by death.

One of the thieves added his scorn to those of the crowd. He spoke insultingly: "Are you not the Christ? Save yourself and us." He expected no help. Perhaps he hoped to ease his torture by heaping ridicule upon the one who was a victim with him.

The kind of affront to God in which men mouth a prayer, but expect no response, is often heard among those whose faith has been ebbed away. It was the insulting cry of a young mother who was close to death. "Why don't you call upon your God?" she cried; "maybe he isn't there." God may have been straining at that moment to help her, but she would have nothing to do with him. Her mind was set in a pattern of doubt.

Much of the seeming lack of response to prayer is explained by the doubts in the mind of the one who prays. The skeptic may say, "Save thyself and us," but the words are a mockery because he does not expect God to help him.

The other thief responded with words of rebuke. Something had happened in the short hours since he was dragged before the tribunal and there sentenced to death. Perhaps it began when he observed Christ's calm demeanor before Pilate, answering the charges against him so effectively that only a greed for popular favor could have allowed the Roman to make such a travesty of justice. The change may have come during the long journey to the summit of Calvary. The thief had found time to turn his eyes toward the strange man who was the central figure in the procession. Perhaps the change came when Jesus spoke the words of forgiveness.

This criminal silenced the cries of the one on the other side of Jesus. He did not claim innocence, nor did he attempt to throw the blame for their plight upon others. "We indeed are suffering justly, for we are receiving due requital." Then his head turned slowly so he could look into the face of Christ.

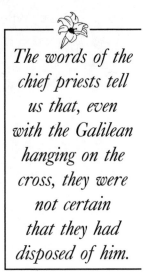

The words of the chief priests tell us that, even with the Galilean hanging on the cross, they were not certain that they had disposed of him.

"Jesus, remember me when you come into your kingdom," he pleaded.

The narrative in Luke indicates that the Master replied immediately. He took no time to contemplate the proper answer. His response was direct and clear.

"I tell you a solemn truth," Jesus said. "Today shalt thou be with me in paradise."

These words are startling. They seem at first a denial of divine justice. But listen again. Think what the words mean to each of us. There is hope here beyond all our dreams.

—G. ERNEST THOMAS
From *Daily Meditations on the
Seven Last Words*

Two Others, on Either Side

If I only had not chanced
    To come upon the way,
Where the bloody crosses branched
    In a fading day;

Had I only heard the tale,
    From mouth to mouth, of One
Dying by a bloody nail
    In a bloody sun—

I would never have the grim
    Haunting eyes to see;
Only the good eyes of him,
    Looking down at me;
I would never find the thief
    Where the saint has trod,
Trace a devil's harsh belief
    In a creed of God;

I could lift a gilded cup,
Snowy bread and wine,
Never asking, as I sup:
"Is this mine?"

—EDITH MIRICK
From *Christ in Poetry*

Lord, When Thy Kingdom Comes

"Lord, when Thy kingdom comes,
remember me";
Thus spake the dying lips to dying ears;
O faith, which in that darkest hour could not see
The promised glory of the far off years!

No kingly sign declares that glory now,
No ray of hope light up that awful hour;
A thorny crown surrounds the bleeding brow,
The hands are stretched in weakness, not in power.

Yet hear the word the dying Savior saith,
"Thou too shalt rest in Paradise today";
O words of life to answer words of faith!
O words of hope for those who live to pray!

Lord, when with dying lips my prayer is said,
Grant that in faith Thy kingdom may I see;
And, thinking on Thy cross and bleeding head,
May breath my parting words, "Remember me."

Remember me, but not my shame or sin;
Thy cleansing blood hath washed them all away;

Thy precious death for me did pardon win;
Thy blood redeemed me in that awful day.

Remember me, and ere I pass away,
Speak Thou th'assuring word that sets us free,
And make Thy promise to my heart, "Today
Thou too shalt rest in Paradise with Me."

—WILLIAM D. MACLAGEN
From *Hymns Ancient and Modern*

CHAPTER SIX

The Darkness

The Darkness

MARK 15:33
  [33]*Now when the sixth hour had come, there was darkness over the whole land until the ninth hour.*

Alas! and Did My Saviour Bleed

Alas! and did my Saviour bleed
And did my Sovereign die?
Would He devote that sacred head
For sinners such as I?
[originally, *For such a worm as I?*]

Refrain
At the cross, at the cross where I first saw the light,
And the burden of my heart rolled away,
It was there by faith I received my sight,
And now I am happy all the day!

Thy body slain, sweet Jesus, Thine—
And bathed in its own blood—
While the firm mark of wrath divine,
His Soul in anguish stood.

Was it for crimes that I had done
He groaned upon the tree?

Amazing pity! Grace unknown!
And love beyond degree!

Well might the sun in darkness hide
And shut his glories in,
When Christ, the mighty Maker died,
For man the creature's sin.

Thus might I hide my blushing face
While His dear cross appears,
Dissolve my heart in thankfulness,
And melt my eyes to tears.

But drops of grief can ne'er repay
The debt of love I owe:
Here, Lord, I give my self away
'Tis all that I can do.

—Isaac Watts

Et Resurrexit Tertia Die
(*Bach,* Credo, *B-minor Mass)*

Three short days of twilight and darkness,
dawn and the light. The elements, free
of all knowledge, unblessed by prediction, yet sensed the
suspense—
Creator entombed by creation, the loftiest heights
brought low, the universe madly askew. Three
short days with the length of three endless nights.

Three times, forced by its nature to shine
the sun reluctantly rose. In the skies no sign
through clouds of a bow. The earth which knew not how

its Maker turned Captive had been yet felt the wrong.
The winds whistled dirges. Three endless
Days—then the groan of creation exploded in song.

> —MARK A. NOLL
> From *A Widening Light: Poems of the Incarnation*

Quote

"The power of the cross of Christ has filled the world."

> —ATHANASIUS OF ALEXANDRIA

Two Crosses

A fiery cross against the night,
Men fleeing, terror-blind—
(The Cross I know means gentleness
Toward all of humankind).

A cross that seeks to purge with flame
The evil from the good—
(The Cross I know brings tolerance
And teaches brotherhood).

This cross rekindles ancient hates
That burned in alien lands—
(The Cross I know is stained with blood
From nail-pierced, holy hands).

> —ADDIE M. HEDRICK
> From *Christ in Poetry*

The Foreigner
(Excerpt)

By noon, the sultry heat has turned to dust storm. The watchers, including the soldiers, appear as shadows. The dispersal of his disciples is echoed by the desertion of the sun. It glows like a fickle moon behind the blackness. In response Jesus utters an enigmatic cry, usually taken to denote at least temporary despair. This may be due to a misunderstanding of what Jesus really said. The two gospel-writers who record it take the cry to be the opening words of the Twenty-Second Psalm: My God, my God, why have you forsaken me? They transliterate the four Aramaic words in Greek letters. Both agree on the last two: *Lema sabachthani?* But their difference transliterations of the first two words—*eloi eloi* in Mark, *eli eli* in Matthew—are curiously balanced by their agreement that bystanders understood Jesus to have called, not on God, but on Elias, or Elijah. One early gospel manuscript has yet another interpretation which one major New Testament textual critic has accepted. This manuscript has the bystanders taking Jesus to be calling on Helios, not Elias. The vocative of Helios—or Elios in the common pronunciation—is Elie. In that case what Jesus cried has been re-interpreted by Christian tradition. If Jesus, at the climax of his life, was showing either an ironic ability to react, to the last, to the world of nature, or affinities to the cosmic view of the Hellenistic Levant, he would have been using, as was not uncommon, Greek and Aramaic in one sentence to cry:

O Sun! O Sun! Why have you forsaken me?

Worn by every form of exhaustion, he let his head slump forward. The rays on his tawdry crown were all that was left to lighten the scene and the scene was dark.

—DESMOND STEWART

> *Worn by every form of exhaustion, Jesus let his head slump forward.*

Before Easter

Spring;
yet frost still builds
dead palaces.

We hear the crack from
icicles of bone,
snow crowns
have snapped the throats
of daffodils,
the ice-queen walks in
her brittle dress.

No rose-blood in the stem,
no cumulus
perfume in the trees,
each day
is a coffin of glass.

The sun is turned
to crystal,
it is our alchemy of winter;
inner cold.

Christ sleeps
behind the quickening stone.

—ISOBEL THRILLING
From *The Lion Christian
Poetry Collection*

ISOBEL THRILLING—In an interview with Resurgence Magazine (May/June 2001), Isobel Thrilling said, "I am particularly interested in science, especially quantum physics, which is very exciting just now with its possibilities and implications. As a non-scientist I can't have access to scientific mechanisms, the formulas and calculations: what is often referred to as 'hard science.' Neither can I have an understanding of mathematical intuitions; they are not available to me because I lack the necessary knowledge. However, I can try to understand the scientific ideas which emerge from behind the 'hardware.' I am deeply indebted to science writers for opening up such areas and providing illumination for the general reader. Art, religion and science all push at the edges of awareness and produce their own revelations which can be shared. God is as natural as electricity."

The Darkness of Moral Despair
(Excerpt)

The three hours of darkness which seem to have culminated the physical aspects of the crucifixion of Jesus have always been deeply symbolic to the devout watchers who gather around the cross of Jesus on the anniversary of his death. Some have felt them to be descriptive of a physical eclipse such as might easily have escaped recording in other sources. Then they have read into this eclipse a symbolic representation of the feelings of shame which a personified nature must have felt at the cruel and unjust death of its creator. It is out of such a concept of the three hours of darkness that we sing

> *Well might the sun in darkness hide*
> *And shut his glories in,*
> *When Christ, the mighty Maker, died*
> *For man the creature's sin.*
> —ISAAC WATTS

But such a conception is really impossible, for the death of Jesus occurred at the time of the Passover. And the fact that the Passover season coincides with the time of full moon renders such an eclipse a physical impossibility.

Some have felt that these hours of darkness were the fulfillment of the words in which Jesus, standing before the Sanhedrin, had uttered: "This is your hour, and the power of darkness." Such an interpretation conceives of the darkness as the release, for the moment, of the powers of darkness and of hell, to wreak their vengeance upon the head of their enemy. Moreover, Jesus had said in the upper room, "Father, save me from this hour: but for this cause came I to this hour." This was the supreme hour for which Jesus had come into the world. It was in this dread hour that the strength of the love of God and the sin of man was to be tried; and in this hour—thanks be to God, who giveth us the victory—victory remained with love. In support of this view there are some who quote that inarticulate cry which Luke tells us the hour of darkness pressed from the lips of Jesus—the cry of a soul face to face with great horror.

> *Jesus had said in the upper room, "Father, save me from this hour: but for this cause came I to this hour."*

But no matter what interpretation we may place upon these three hours of darkness, we who are watching at the cross realize that they did bring from the lips of Jesus this fourth word, a cry of moral despair, in the realization of the separation from God which the darkness symbolized.

—WILLIAM C. SKEATH
From *His Last Words*

Plain Fact

The winter cold
has not yet left my bones.
I shiver in this birthing Spring's

first light.
No sun, no shadow,
only the truth
of tree and slated sky.
Though no bird sings,
with certitude I brace
against the failing chill,
awaiting Easter.

> —MYRNA REID GRANT
> From *A Widening Light:*
> *Poems of the Incarnation*

Easter

All night had shout . . . .
Of woeful women, . . . this way;
Until that noon of somber sky
On Friday, clamour and display
Smote him; no solitude had he,
No silence, since Gethsemane.

Public was Death; but Power, but Might,
But Life again, but Victory,
Were hushed within the dead of night,
The shuttered dark, the secrecy.
And all alone, alone, alone
He rose again behind the stone.

> —ALICE MEYNELL
> From *The Lion Christian*
> *Poetry Collection*

The Greatest Story Ever Told
(Excerpt)

The slowly darkening indigo sky was losing its deep violet blue and turning to black. The agony of the gentle prisoner, the memory of His good works, the wailing of the women all helped to change the mood of the watchers. Twice He had spoken from the cross: once to pray for the soldiers even at the very moment they were enforcing the tent pegs through His hands; and again when He spoke to His mother.

The storm was gathering its darkness now; the air of the black sirocco was getting murkier by the minute with a wrack of clouds and dark floating vapor scudding across the sky. There was a low, rolling sound of thunder, a rumble swelling to roar and crash over the heads of the people. As the rain came, many scattered, but others remained, to miss nothing. Even the most vociferous of the paid mob began to feel a germ of fear. The sun was lost behind the thickening nimbus overhead and there was a low and constant murmuring among the people. Tumult and panic were ready to break out into mob madness. This, they began to fear, was no ordinary storm; this was not the familiar black sirocco which came to Jerusalem each year at the beginning of April. This was a brooding, deepening, lightless storm of sinister intensity.

—Fulton Oursler

Easter Saturday

A curiously empty day.
As if the world's life
Had gone underground.
The April sun

Warming dry grass
Makes pale spring promises
But nothing comes to pass.

Anger
Relaxes into despair
As we remember our helplessness,
Remember him hanging there.
We have purchased the spices
But they must wait for tomorrow.
We shall keep today
For emptiness and sorrow.

—ELIZABETH ROONEY
From *The Lion Christian
Poetry Collection*

The Darkness of Golgotha

*From the sixth hour there was darkness over all the land until the ninth
hour.*

—MATTHEW 27:45

There's always the danger that we might read this verse too quickly.
We treat it too often as though it were merely the record of something
incidental.

As a matter of fact, it is the central verse in the story of the cross.
Indeed, the cross itself is not mentioned in the verse—no word is spoken
of it or of the Christ. They are alike hidden, and yet the period was
one of three hour's duration, the very central hours of the experience of
the Savior of men. Christ and the cross are alike hidden within that verse,
and that fact is most suggestive because in those hours transactions were
accomplished that through all eternity defy the apprehension and explanation of finite minds.

It is not to be passed over lightly that all the Synoptists record the fact of that darkness. Three hours of darkness and of silence! All the ribald clamor was over, the material opposition utterly exhausted, the turmoil ended. Man had done his last and his worst. Beyond that period of the three hours' silence, even human actions were expressive of pity. Nothing has impressed my own heart, or amazed me more in reading this story anew, and attempting to meditate upon it in view of this service, than what I shall venture to describe as the wonderful psychological conditions of those hours beyond the hours of silence.

It is as though that appalling silence and that overwhelming darkness had changed the entire attitude of man to the Savior. The very vinegar they offered Him to drink was offered Him in pity. What they said about Elijah was expressive of their desire to sympathize. The centurion's testimony was that of a man whose heart was strangely moved toward the august and dignified Savior. When presently they found Him dead, and therefore did not break His bones, the spear thrust was one of kindness, lest perchance He might still suffer, in spite of the fact that He appeared to be dead. Multitudes dispersed from the scene at Golgotha smiting their breasts, overwhelmed with a sense of awe, and strangely moved by some new pity. And there is no picture in all the New Testament more full of pathos and of power than that of the women standing silent and amazed through all those hours of His suffering, and still standing there beyond them.

> *At last the words spoken of the final committal, full of dignity, were spoken: "Father, into Thy hands I commend My spirit."*

Then also all of the cries that passed the lips of Jesus beyond the darkness were significant. "My God! My God, why didst Thou forsake Me! (Matthew 27:46)—for that was the tense; a slight change from the tense of the actual Psalm, a question asked by One who was emerging from the experience to which He referred. And then as John is most careful to record for us, "Knowing that all things were now finished, He said, I thirst" (John 19:28). Beyond that came the words of the great proclamation, "It is finished" (John 19:30). And at last the words spoken of the final committal, full of dignity, were spoken: "Father, into Thy hands I commend My spirit" (Luke 23:46). Everything was changed beyond the hours of silence and of darkness.

Much has been written about these hours of darkness, much which is not warranted by any careful spiritual attention to the story itself. You will call to mind how, at great length many years ago, it was argued that the darkness was that of the sun's eclipse. But that is entirely impossible, for Passover was always held at full moon, when there could be no eclipse of the sun. The darkness has been described as nature's sympathy with the suffering of the Lord, but that is a pagan conception of nature, a conception of nature as having some consciousness apart from God and out of harmony with His work. It has been said that the darkness was brought about by an act of God, and was expressive of His sympathy with His Son. I admit that that is an appealing idea, and has some element of truth in it, in that we may discover the overruling of His government; but to declare that that darkness was caused by God because of His sympathy with His Son is to deny the cry of Jesus which immediately followed the darkness and referred to it. The darkness was to Him a period when He experienced whatever He may have meant by the words, "Thou didst forsake Me" (Matthew 27:46).

> *Did any word escape His lips that will help us to explain those silent hours?*

If I have succeeded in these words spoken in reverent spirit, in suggesting to you the difficulty of those central three hours, then our hearts are prepared for going forward.

I submit thoughtfully that no interpretation of that darkness is to be trusted save that of the Lord who experienced it. Has He flung any light on the darkness which will enable us to apprehend the meaning of the darkness? Did any word escape His lips that will help us to explain those silent hours? I think the answer is to be found in these narratives, and to that teaching of the Lord we appeal in order that we may consider the meaning of the darkness, and the passing of the darkness, and thereafter attempt reverently to look back at the transaction in the darkness.

—GEORGE CAMPBELL MORGAN
From *Classic Sermons on the Cross of Christ*

Easter Midnight Service

A pagan fire to conjure in the spring—
But this fire we have lit to conjure out
The winter chill of all the pagan rout,
And conjure in the summer of the king.
Soon will the brazen bells of triumph ring,
And midnight dark be shaken by a shout
That death's cold chain that gripped the world about
Is broken link from link: and the links sing.

And fire from fire our candles take the light,
As we take fire from the eternal flame,
And flame from flame we walk down the dark aisle,
Each flame a glory gold against the night,
That trembles at the whisper of the name
That burns through the empty halls of hell.

—MARION PITMAN
From *The Lion Christian
Poetry Collection*

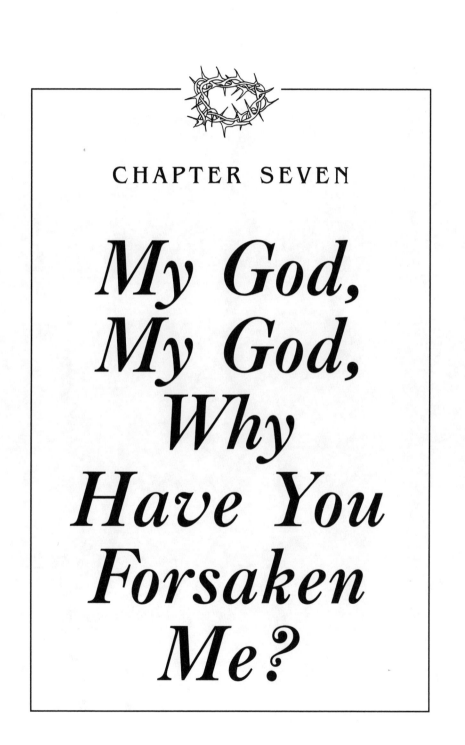

CHAPTER SEVEN

My God, My God, Why Have You Forsaken Me?

CHAPTER · SEVEN

My God, My God, Why Have You Forsaken Me?

ARK 15:34
[34]And at the ninth hour Jesus cried out with a loud voice, saying, "Eloi, Eloi, lama sabachthani?" which is translated, "My God, My God, why have You forsaken Me?"

His Last Words
(Excerpt)

When the night of death was falling
On the brow of Calvary,
Jesus cried to God in anguish:
"Why hast thou forsaken me?"
In that bitter hour the Savior
Touched the depth of human woe,
So that he might be a brother
To the lowest of the low.

But his God had not forsaken:
He was still beside the Son;
Closer he than John or Mary,
Arms of love about his own.
Grace he gave him to endure it,
Strength to conquer death and hell,

Till he won eternal triumph,
Then went up to heaven to dwell.

God still dwells in clouds and darkness,
Shadows hide from sight his face;
But his love is ever present,
Never failing in his grace;
If we share the Saviour's sorrow,
We shall also share his love;
If we bear his cross of service,
We shall reign with him above.

—UNKNOWN

Anno Domini MCMXVII

You have stopped beating the drums
with a dying fall on all horizons
behind flag-draped coffins, stopped
giving up wounds and tears to pity
in the razed cities, ruin on ruin.
And no one cries any longer "O God why hast
thou forsaken me?" No milk
nor blood flows any more from the riddled breast.
Now you have hidden the guns among the magnolias,
leave us one day without arms, on the grass
with the sound of moving water
and fresh leaves of cane in our hair
while we clasp the woman who loves us.
At nightfall sound no sudden
curfew. A day, a single
day for ourselves, O lords of the earth,

before once again air and metal heave
and a splinter catches us full in the face.

> —SALVATORE QUASIMODO, translated
> from the Italian by Jack Bevan
> From *The Gospels in Our Image*

SALVATORE QUASIMODO (1901–1968)—Italian poet, Salvatore Quasimodo, received the Nobel Laureate in Literature in 1959 for his lyrical poetry about the tragedy of life. He worked with the Italian government's civil engineering corps until 1938, when he left to become the editor of the weekly magazine, *Tempo*. He received many literary prizes during his life, including the Etna-Taormina International Prize in Poetry that he shared with Dylan Thomas. His works have been translated into 40 languages, and his son, Alessandro, a noted actor and director, travels the world reciting his father's poetry.

Crucifixion

*"Do not weep for me, Mother,
when I am in my grave."*

I.
A choir of angels glorified the hour,
the vault of heaven was dissolved in fire.
"Father, why hast Thou forsaken me?
Mother, I beg you, do not weep for me . . ."

II.
Mary Magdalene beat her breasts and sobbed,
His dear disciple, stone-faced, stared.
His mother stood apart. No other looked
into her secret eyes. Nobody dared.

> —ANNA AKHMATOVA, translated from
> the Russian by Stanley Kunitz
> and Max Hayward
> From *The Gospels in Our Image*

Eloi, Eloi, Lama Sabachthani?

How I hate myself, this body which is me;
How it dogs me, what a galling shadow!
How I would like to cut off my hands,
And take out my intestines to torture them!

But I can't, for it is written against me I must not,
I must preserve my life from hurt.

But then, that shadow's shadow of me,
The enemy!

God, how glad I am to hear the shells
Droning over, threatening me!
It is their threat, their loud, jeering threat,
Like screaming birds of Fate
Wheeling to lacerate and rip up this my body,
It is the loud cries of these birds of pain
That gives me peace.

For I hate this body, which is so dear to me:
My legs, my breast, my belly:
My God, what agony they are to me;
For I dote on them with tenderness, and I hate them,
I hate them bitterly.

My God, that they should always be with me!
Nay, now at last thank God for the jeopardy,
For the shells, that the question is now no more before me.

I do not die, I am not even hurt,
But I kill my shadow's shadow of me!

And God is good, yes, God is very good!
I shot my man, I saw him crumble and hang
A moment as he fell—and grovel, and die.

And God is good, for I wanted him to die,
To twist, and grovel, and become a heap of dirt
In death. This death, his death, my death—
It is the same, this death.

So when I run at length thither across
To the trenches, I see again a face with blue eyes,
A blanched face, fixed and agonized,
Waiting. And I knew he wanted it.
Like a bride he took my bayonet, wanting it,
Like a virgin the blade of my bayonet, wanting it,
And it sank to rest from me in him,
And I, the lover, am consummate,
And he is the bride, I have sown him with the seed
And planted and fertilized him.

But what are you, woman, peering through the rents
In the purple veil?
Would you peep in the empty house like a pilferer?
You are mistaken, the veil of the flesh is rent
For the Lord to come forth at large, on the scent of blood,
Not for the thieves to enter, the pilferers.

Is there no reconciliation?
Is marriage only with death?
In death the consummation?
What I beget, must I beget of blood?
Are the guns and the steel the bridegroom,
Our flesh the bride?

I had dreamed of love, oh love, I had dreamed of love,
And the veil of the temple rent at the kiss on kiss.

And God revealed through the sweat and the heat of love,
And God abroad and alight on us everywhere,
Everywhere men and women alight with God,
My body glad as the bell of a flower
And hers a flowerbell swinging
In a breeze of knowledge.

Why should we hate, then, with this hate incarnate?
Why am I bridegroom of War, war's paramour?
What is the crime, that my seed is turned to blood,
My kiss to wounds?
Who is it will have it so, who did the crime?
And why do the women follow us satisfied,
Feed on our wounds like bread, receive our blood
Like glittering seed upon them for fulfillment?

Lord, what we have done we hereby expiate.
We expiate in our bodies' rents and rags
In our sheaf or self-gathered wounds: we go to meet
Our bride among the rustling chorus of shells,
Whose birds they are,
We give up, O Lord, our bodies to deadly hate,
We take the bride, O God, and our seed of life
Runs richly from us.
We expiate it thus, the unknowable crime,
We give hate her dues, O God, we yield her up
Our bodies to the expiation, Lord.

But shall I touch hands with death in killing that other,
The enemy, my brother?
Shall I offer him my brotherly body to kill,
Be bridegroom or best man, as the case turns out?

The odds are even and he will have it so.
It may be I shall give the bride

And the marriage shall be my brother's—it may be so—
I walk the earth intact hereafterwards;
The crime full-expiate, the Erinnyes sunk
Like blood in the earth again; we walk the earth
Unchallenged, intact, unabridged, henceforth a host
Cleansed and in concord from the bed of death.

—D. H. LAWRENCE
From *The Gospels in Our Image*

D. H. LAWRENCE (1885–1930)—D. H. Lawrence was the inexhaustible author of poems, novels, short stories, plays, essays, and criticism. His works were influenced by his early years in Nottinghamshire, where he was the fourth child of Arthur Lawrence and Lydia Beardsall. His adult career began as a clerk for a surgical appliance manufacturer. He began teaching in 1902 and retired due to illness in 1912. He married Frieda Weekley in 1914 and the two traveled extensively until his death on March 2, 1930 in the south of France.

"Why Hast Thou Forsaken Me?"
(Psalm 22:1)

Perhaps the Socrates he had never read,
The Socrates that Socrates poorly understood,
Had the answer. From opposites, opposites
Are generated. Cold to heat, heat to cold,
Life to death, and death to life. Perhaps the grave's
Obscenity is the womb, the only one
For the glorified body. It may be
Darkness alone, darkness black and mute,
Void of God and a human smile, filled
With hateful laughter, dirty jokes, rattling dice,
Can empty the living room of all color

Or perhaps, being man, it was simply
He must first go wherever man had been,
To whatever caves of loneliness, whatever
Caverns of no light, deep damp darkness,
Dripping walls of the spirit, man has known.

I have called to God and heard no answer,
I have seen the thick curtain drop, and sunlight die;
My voice has echoed back, a foolish voice,
The prayer restored intact to its silly source.
I have walked in darkness, he hung in it.
In all of my mines of night, he was there first;
In whatever dead tunnel I am lost, he finds me.
My God, My God, why hast thou forsaken me?
From his perfect darkness a voice says, I have not.

—CHAD WALSH
From *A Widening Light:*
Poems of the Incarnation

The Saviour Speaks
(13th Century)

Thou who createdst everything,
Sweet Father, heavenly King,
Hear me—I, thy son, implore:
For Man this flesh and bone I bore.

Clear and bright my breast and side,
Blood over whiteness spilling wide,
Holes in my body crucified.

Stiff and stark my long arms rise,
Dimness and darkness cloud my eyes;
Like sculpted marble hang my thighs.

Red my feet with the flowing blood,
Holes in them washed through with that flood.
Mercy on Man's sins, Father on high!
Through all my wounds to thee I cry!

—ANONYMOUS
From *The Lion Christian
Poetry Collection*

The Life of Christ
(Excerpt)

The first three Words were spoken at the beginning of the period during which Jesus hung on the cross; the last four at the end. The first group show His relation to man; the last His relation to His Father.

The wave of hatred and fury against Christ had spent itself in His trial and procession and the first moments of His crucifixion. From then on the crowds began to melt away, for it was Friday of the Paschal Octave, the Parasceve, and a great festival day. Besides, an awesome phenomenon was beginning to make itself felt. At about twelve o'clock, a mysterious darkness began to creep over the earth. At first it did not frighten the throngs on the highway who stood staring up at the three crosses, for they thought it was merely the passing of heavy clouds. But when the sun contracted into a blood-red ball, terror took possession of both the multitude on the hill and the people in the city. Birds and beasts took to cover. A heavy silence fell over all.

> *A mysterious darkness began to creep over the earth.*

For three hours the darkness increased. As the light faded, the rabble fled. The soldiers were nodding from the drinks which they had taken immediately after the crucifixion. The two thieves were growing confused and insensible from their pain. Of Christ's enemies only a few of the more calloused members of the Sanhedrin remained near His cross. The three Marys and John kept their station.

Then, toward the ninth hour, Jesus Himself broke the silence. The night that had descended on the earth was but a symbol of another mysterious darkness that had crept over the soul of our Savior, the desolation of being forsaken by the Father. This was the realization of what He had feared in Gesthsemane. The very thought of it had forced drops of blood from His body; now its actuality wrings words of anguish from His lips.

"*Eli, Eli, lamma sabacthani?*" He cried in a loud voice. "That is, My God, My God, why hast Thou forsaken Me?"

Jesus was not abandoned, of course, in the absolute or dogmatic sense of the word, since by His Divine Nature He was one with the Father; but at the moment of His cry the full current of God's wrath for all the sins of mankind flowed through His tortured soul, to make His body surge against the nails and to force the cry of abysmal anguish from His lips. The Father abandoned Him for a short time to the concentrated suffering of complete atonement for us all. Such a moment had been prophesied centuries before, in the Twenty-first Psalm, the first words of which Jesus uttered in His cry.

His words ringing through the darkness reached the ears of remaining members of the Sanhedrin. "This Man calleth Elias," said some . . .

—Isidore O'Brien

The Screwtape Letters
(Excerpt)

. . . One must face the fact that all the talk about His love for men, and His service being perfect freedom, is not (as one would gladly believe) mere propaganda, but an appalling truth. He really does want to fill the universe with a lot of loathsome little replicas of Himself—creatures whose life, on its miniature scale, will be qualitatively like His own, not because He has absorbed them but because their wills freely conform to His. We want cattle who can finally become food; He wants servants who can finally become sons. We want to suck in, He wants to give out. We are empty and would be filled; He is full and flows over. Our war aim is a world in which Our Father Below has drawn all other beings into himself: the Enemy wants a world full of beings united to Him but still distinct.

> *The Enemy wants a world full of beings united to Him but still distinct.*

And that is where the troughs come in. You must have often wondered why the Enemy does not make more use of His power to be sensibly present to human souls in any degree He chooses and at any moment. But you now see that the Irresistible and the Indisputable are the two weapons which the very nature of His scheme forbids Him to use. Merely to override a human will (as His felt presence in any but the faintest and most mitigated degree would certainly do) would be for Him useless. He cannot ravish. He can only woo. For His ignoble idea is to eat the cake and have it; the creatures are to be one with Him, but yet themselves; merely to cancel them, or assimilate them, will not serve. He is prepared to do a little overriding at the beginning. He will set them off with communications of His presence which, though faint, seem great to them, with emotional sweetness, and easy conquest over temptation. But He never allows this state of affairs to last long. Sooner or later He withdraws, if not in fact, at least from their conscious experience, all those supports and incentives. He leaves the creature to stand up on its own legs—to carry out from the will alone duties which have lost all relish. It is during such trough periods, much more than during peak periods, that it is growing into the sort of creature He wants it to be. Hence the prayers offered in the state of dryness are those which please Him best. We can drag our patients along by continual tempting, because we design them only for the table, and the more their will is interfered with, the better. He cannot "tempt" to virtue as we do to vice. He wants them to learn to walk and must therefore take away His hand; and if only the will to walk is really there He is pleased even with their stumbles. Do not be deceived, Wormwood. Our cause is never more in danger than when a human, no longer desiring, but still intending, to do our Enemy's will, looks round upon a universe from which every trace of Him seems to have vanished, and asks why he has been forsaken, and still obeys . . .

—C. S. Lewis

The Darkness of Moral Despair
(Excerpt)

It is indeed an awful thing, possibly beyond our human comprehension, to be shut out from all that is pure and good. We have seen the look of despair which comes with the knowledge of the futility of further effort. I remember standing by a mother when the physician told her nothing more could be done to help the child she loved. Through an agony of weeks that mother had carefully nursed her sick daughter. And now, in spite of the long hours of anxious watching, in spite of the painful moments of sacrificial effort, the physician was telling her of the futility of all further effort—the child could not recover. We know, indeed, something of the despair of futility.

> *Music played by an orchestra vibrates life and laughter.*

We have seen the despair of a wasted life. In the evening the great house is a blaze of light in preparation for the feast. Fresh flowers are on every stand; the house is filled with the fragrance of their perfume. The tables, laded as they are with fruits and viands, are beautiful to behold. The music played by the orchestra vibrates life and laughter. But wait! Wait until the morning hours have come, when the feast is over and the revelers are gone! The flowers are drooping dejectedly in the stifled air. The candles have finally sputtered out in their socket.

The music has died away; only torn and scattered pages lie where the musicians have thrown them. The guests have gone; the air is foul. And there, amid the ruins of the feast, the blear-eyed, befuddled reveler, whose life is almost done, sits alone. Yes, we know something of the despair of a life wasted as the Prodigal wasted life.

Yet the despairing of the mother can be cheered with the thought of a reunion. The heart of the reveler may yet assert its manhood and use life's few remaining moments to recoup a wasted fortune. But who can conceive the blackness of despair of a soul forever shut out from all that is good? It is this which Jesus is suffering. He knows the despair of having his teachings rejected by the Jewish leaders. How his tender heart must have been cut to the quick as they turned from him, these intellectuals, with supercilious sneers at the statements of God's love for men, and with the jeering word "Galilean" on their tongues. He knew the sadness of having the multitude at first hang on his every word, then turn against him as they sought other supplies of costless loaves and fishes. He knew the anguish of being deserted by the ones he loved, and of the final traitorous kiss

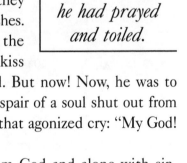

Jesus knew the anguish of being deserted by the ones he loved, and of the final traitorous kiss of one for whom he had prayed and toiled.

of one for whom he had prayed and toiled. But now! Now, he was to experience the depth of all despair—the despair of a soul shut out from God. That forever must be the meaning of that agonized cry: "My God! My God! Why hast *thou* forsaken me?"

It is an awful thing to be shut out from God and alone with sin. Moses seemed alone when he led the children of Israel, when he saw the fretful fickleness in the hearts of those for whom he toiled, or the hateful cunning in the eyes of Pharaoh. But he only seemed to be alone—God was with him! Elijah seemed alone when on the summit of Carmel he confronted the hideous idolatry of the priests of Baal, when he fled in terror from the hatred of Ahab and Jezebel. But neither was he alone— God was with him! But to be shut out from the very face of God by human sin, with no ear into which one can pour a confession, and no heart to which one can go for sympathy—who can conceive the tragedy of the despair of such a soul?

In The Marble Faun Hawthorne tells us the story of a young girl, raised in New England, with a Protestant religious background, and a rich but strict Puritan heritage of training. While on a visit to Rome, unwittingly she sees a horrible crime committed. Well, what of that? Simply this: for one moment she has looked into hell, and the sight will give her no rest—no rest, indeed, until, Protestant to the core though she is, she pours out her tale in the ear of a priest. Jesus was now looking at sin in its worst awfulness, was staring wide-eyed into the mysteries of hell. Even now, with the awful desolation of soul that comes from a clear glimpse of sin, he was shut out from the face of God himself. Can we wonder at that burst of agony: "My God! Why hast *thou* forsaken me?

> *The priest laid his hands upon the goat, and pronounced that all the sins of the assembled worshipers had been placed upon the head of the goat.*

Connected with the Day of Atonement in the old Mosaic ritual was a ceremony of very deep significance. It was a banishing of the scapegoat. In the presence of the assembled people, the priest took the goat, laid his hands upon it, and pronounced that all the sins of the assembled worshipers had been placed upon the head of the goat. Then the goat was driven out from the congregation as an accursed thing—out into the desert to die of hunger and thirst. There is, by the way, a very deep meaning in that later cry, "I thirst." Jesus was in fact the scape-goat of humanity. Upon him were piled high— mountain high—the sins of men. All the sins of adulterous, untruthful, murderous humanity, ungrateful to God and hateful of goodness, were laid upon his head. He was driven, so to speak, like the scape-goat out from the presence of God into the desert of sin to die of hunger and thirst and of the wrath of God.

Thus Jesus tastes the sorrow of spiritual death for all men. He meets the last enemy of humanity and feels the sting of death. The serpent of sin is bruising the heel of the seed of the woman. . . . This we believe to be the real meaning of that inarticulate cry which Luke tells us the darkness forced from the lips of Jesus. He was, in this darkness, experiencing the horror of passing into the very power of hell. But the heel of the seed of the woman is to bruise the head of the serpent; and after that inarticulate cry, Luke can tell us that he quietly uttered the "It is finished!" of his triumph.

—WILLIAM C. SKEATH
From *His Last Words*

God as Seen in Christ

God was in Christ! That is the central fact in the Christian gospel. The teachings of Jesus during his public ministry reveal the truth. The transcendent nature of that revelation is evident in the Crucifixion. God was at work in Christ during the long hours when he hung in helpless agony.

An impressive picture of Calvary can be seen in the National Gallery in London. Christ is on the cross, almost hidden in the darkness. At first the one who looks observes nothing but the blackness and through it the dim figure of the suffering Christ. But if his gaze does not falter, he glimpses a figure with arms outstretched, tenderly holding up the suffering one. His face is twisted by a pain which is more agonizing even than that of the Christ. God the Father is grieving with his Son as he hangs on the cross.

> *Through the blackness, we can see God the Father in all His agony, tenderly holding up His Son and grieving with Him as He hangs on the cross.*

When the Words spoken by Jesus on Calvary are examined in the light of the fact that God was revealing his nature by the events which occurred that day, they assume a significance which is timeless. It is possible to analyze and weigh them with a view to finding a key to the heart and mind of God.

A panorama of eternal significance unfolds before the eyes of those who long to know the truth.

The Fourth Word came out of the abject misery of continued pain. "My God, my God, why hast thou forsaken me?" cried the Christ.

At first these words seem completely human. They appear to be a desperate question which was born out of unrelieved agony. Many scholars have been satisfied to let them remain an evidence that even Christ experienced a moment when the face of his Father was blotted out.

> *The cause of Jesus' cry was loneliness and was prompted by suffering and a heart that was breaking.*

It is reasonable to accept such an interpretation when we are searching for an answer to human pain in the words of Jesus. A cry of loneliness is understandable even when it comes from the lips of the most courageous of men.

Eternal truth was revealed on Calvary. The words of Jesus have a divine as well as human message for humanity. What, then, can we learn from the Fourth Word?

Remember that God was in Christ, bearing all the agony accompanying the most cruel form of death known to man. God was feeling the pain. God in Christ was speaking words which were fraught with eternal meaning. Already he had declared that forgiveness is an attribute of the divine nature, already he had opened the portals of heaven for repentant souls in every generation, and he had lifted the family to an exalted place in the divine plan. When he uttered the Fourth Word, he was revealing another truth of everlasting significance.

The form of expression is less important than the truth it suggests. "My God, my God, why hast thou forsaken me?" The question is from the first verse of the twenty-second psalm, a familiar passage to every faithful servant of Jehovah. It originally represented the pitiful cry of people who were oppressed by a conqueror. The tyrant had destroyed their holy places and had carried away the flower of their youth into slavery.

The heart of the cry is loneliness. It was prompted by suffering and heartbreak. When God in Christ used these words, he was revealing something about the divine nature which man has seldom understood. It tells us that God suffers! It reminds us that God is sometimes lonely! It announces that God's heart is often broken!

—G. Ernest Thomas
From *Daily Meditations on
the Seven Last Words*

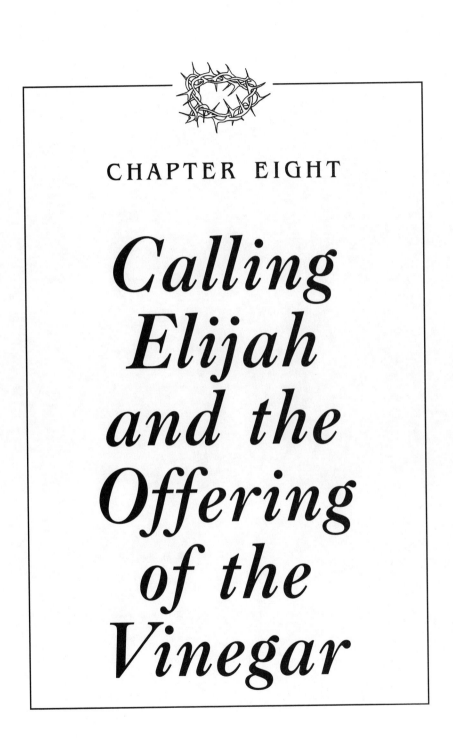

CHAPTER EIGHT

Calling Elijah and the Offering of the Vinegar

Calling Elijah and the Offering of the Vinegar

MATTHEW 27:47–49

[47] Some of those who stood there, when they heard that, said, "This Man is calling for Elijah!" [48] Immediately one of them ran and took a sponge, filled it with sour wine and put it on a reed, and offered it to Him to drink. [49] The rest said, "Let Him alone; let us see if Elijah will come to save Him."

The Cup

If now unto my lips be raised
   The brimming cup of bitter gall,
Grant Thy great strength, dear Lord, and I
   Will drink it all.

My lips may quiver, and my faint heart quail,
   And I may cry at its dread call;
Hold Thou my hand, dear Lord, and I
   Will drink it all.

—FREDERICK T. ROBERTS
From *Christ in Poetry*

The Life of Christ
(Excerpt)

"*Eli, Eli, lamma sabacthani?*" He cried in a loud voice. "That is, My God, My God, why hast Thou forsaken Me?"

His words ringing through the darkness reached the ears of the remaining members of the Sanhedrin. "This Man calleth Elias," said some; and one of these, in fear and awe at the thought of the great prophet, ran for a sponge and soaked it in water and vinegar, the usual drink of the Roman soldier. While he was doing this Jesus uttered His Fifth Word: "I thirst." This too fulfilled a prophecy: "My tongue hath cleaved to My jaws"; "And in My thirst they gave Me vinegar to drink."

The bystander who had found and filled the sponge with water and vinegar then stuck it on a hyssop reed about two feet long, and approached Jesus with it. But the other hardened enemies of Christ who stood around him said: "Let be, let us see whether Elias will come to deliver Him." The man disregarded their words, however, and wet Jesus' lips.

> *Jesus' words ringing through the darkness reached the ears of the remaining members of the Sanhedrin.*

That incident completed Christ's mortal life. He had fulfilled every task, suffered every pain that the Father had given Him to do and to endure in the Redemption of mankind. All that was needed now to open the gates of heaven was His death, and that He would accomplish by freely and obediently laying down His life. For though Jesus truly died, He did not die as other men do who, owing to natural causes, cannot live any longer. Christ did not die of exhaustion; of His own free will He expired to redeem us. This the Evangelists unmistakably indicate. And Christ Himself had made it clear that He Himself would freely "lay down His life" and "take it up again."

As soon as He tasted the mixture on the sponge, He said: "It is consummated." And then "with a loud voice," to show that the current of life in Him was full and strong, He cried: "Father, into Thy hands I commend My spirit," bowed His head and "gave up the ghost."

—ISIDORE O'BRIEN

VINEGAR—Vinegar was discovered more than 10,000 years ago and has been produced from sour wine, as well as from molasses, fruit, honey, potatoes, and grains—anything that contains sugar. The natural sugars ferment to alcohol, and the alcohol ferments to vinegar. The Babylonians used vinegar as a preservative and condiment, while Romans used it as a beverage. Today, vinegar is used in the kitchen for cooking and for cleaning, but also for rashes and insect bites. Amazingly, the shelf life of vinegar is indefinite.

Crusts

How cruel they! The cause of all
    His anguish—they who gibed and cursed;
Then proffered cup of bitter gall
    To slake his thirst.

Yet we, who set ourselves apart,
    Still nourish sordid greed and lust:
He hungers for a loving heart;
    We fling—a crust.

—WALTER SHEA
From *Christ in Poetry*

A Spiritual Thirst

The careful student of the word of God, finds no reason for surprise in the events leading to the utterance of this fifth word from the cross. Centuries before this moment, the Psalmist had given similar expression.

"My God, my God, why hast thou forsaken me? . . . All they that see me laugh me to scorn: they shoot out the lip, they shake the head, saying, He trusted on the Lord that he would deliver him: let him deliver him, seeing he delighted in him . . . My strength is dried up like a potsherd; and my tongue cleaveth to my jaws; and thou hast brought me into the dust of death . . . They pierced my hands and my feet . . . they look and stare upon me . . . They part my garments among them, and cast lots upon my vesture." When one joins these words, which are taken from the twenty-second Psalm, with words from the sixty-ninth Psalm, "in my thirst they gave me vinegar to drink," one would be rather surprised if Jesus had not cried out, "I thirst," and if some bystander had not handed him a draught of vinegar. We really have been looking for just such a cry, and our expectancy has grown out of the exact way in which every detail of the crucifixion has been provisioned in the sacred writings.

> *No one can question that behind Jesus' request for water, there was a great spiritual purpose.*

In this cry of thirst there is a strange mixture of the human and the divine. It is not the first time that Jesus has craved a drink of cooling water from human hands. There, by the well of Samaria, while waiting for the return of his disciples, Jesus had asked a woman of Samaria for a drink of water. It may well have been that Jesus was thirsty then, and that there was something of a physical background for his request. Yet in the light of subsequent conversation, no one can question that behind his request there was a great spiritual purpose. He was thirsting for a drink of water, yes; but he was thirsting also for the soul of this woman.

So now again, Jesus is thirsting. No doubt at all there is a physical foundation to the cry, "I thirst." He is feeling the thirst of the soldier lying wounded on the battle-field; his fevered body-cells are crying our for water. All this is true; but here again the thought is persistent that the physical thirst is but a fountain for a greater thirst, a spiritual thirst for the souls of men. His ministry began with an expression of physical appetite which was immediately glorified into a spiritual appetite. In his temptation, while his body hungered, his soul fed on the word of God. The record is that he "was afterward an hungred," but that his soul cried

out, "Man shall not live my bread alone!" His ministry now closes with
an equally intense physical appetite, that of thirst. But it is far more than
a thirst for water; it is a consuming thirst after God, a thirst for the souls
of men.

And just as Jesus' prayer for the forgiveness of his tormentors found
an answer in the penitence of the evil-doer, so now his prayer for water
finds a response awakened in the heart of one
who might be least expected to answer that
prayer—in the heart of one of the rough soldiers,
who had laughed as the dice were cast for the
seamless robe.

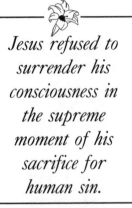

*Jesus refused to
surrender his
consciousness in
the supreme
moment of his
sacrifice for
human sin.*

We must very carefully distinguish this drink
of vinegar from the draught of vinegar and gall
which was offered to Jesus at the moment of his
being nailed to the cross. Jesus had refused that
drink. That mixture of sour wine and opium was
provided by some of the pious women of Jerusa-
lem, to ease the sufferings of the victims of the Roman cross. They did
it, on the sanction of the Rabbis, who thus interpreted Proverbs 31:6, 7.
But then Jesus refused to surrender his consciousness in the supreme
moment of his sacrifice for human sin. It was no stupefied, bewildered
victim who uttered the words to which we have been listening.

The drink of vinegar which was placed upon hyssop and lifted to the
lips of Jesus in answer to his cry of thirst, was something vastly different. "The vinegar of Scripture is wine which has undergone . . . fermen-
tation . . . whereby its alcohol is converted into acetic acid . . . This
fluid was used as a relish . . . Into it food was dipped before eating. A
diluted vinegar or sour wine was used as a drink by the poorer classes,
and especially by soldiers . . . The vessel of vinegar which the Roman
soldiers had by them at the crucifixion was probably filled with this drink,
which was called *posca*. It was not regarded as intoxicating." In other words,
the cry of thirst which came from the lips of Jesus found a response in
the most unexpected place—in the heart of the Roman soldier who has-
tened to share his ration of wine with the sufferer on the cross! In what
strange soil we sometimes find the seeds of God's mercy springing up!

And this cry of Jesus has found a response again in the heart of his church. All our hospitals, crowded as they are with those angels of mercy which we call nurses and physicians, all our orphanages, our homes for the aged, our asylums, our rest homes—what are these but the visualization of the answers to the cry of Jesus for pity upon the sufferings of humanity?

Today we feel again the spiritual implications of that cry. If a rough Roman soldier could be moved by that cry to share his rations with Jesus, shall we refuse to recognize his thirst for our souls? No, rather shall we surrender ourselves to him. As that soldier assuaged his physical thirst, shall we not assuage his spiritual thirst by the surrender of our lives to him?

—WILLIAM C. SKEATH
From *His Last Words*

Good Friday

Gall is the taste of life when we
Who live must bear our Calvary.
On this day our Master died—
Christ, our Lord, the Crucified.
Upon the cross in agony
He shed his blood for love of me.
In every street, on every hill,
The Heart that stopped is beating still.

—VINCENT HOLME
From *Christ in Poetry*

The Fifth Word

Jesus was not ashamed to ask. He had no false pride. He asked. And when the soldiers heard his cry "I thirst," one of them ran. He took a sponge, soaked it with his own ration of sour wine and put it on a reed. He "ran" says scripture, and held it up for Jesus to drink.

"I thirst." Jesus was not ashamed to ask. *Blessed are they which do hunger and thirst after righteousness* (blessed are they who are not ashamed to ask) *for they shall be filled.* Do you remember how desperately Jesus prayed at Gethsemane? "O my Father," he asked, "if it be possible, let this cup pass from me." The cross was a cup of suffering. Jesus *asked* God to take it away. The cross was a cup he did not want to drink. But does not the beatitude say blessed are they which do thirst?

The blessing God gives is not always what we ask.

Put them together, the cross and the beatitude! This is what they mean: The blessing God gives is not always what we ask. Nevertheless, his blessing always satisfies. He fills our hearts to overflowing. *My cup runneth over.*

There is a strange writing. No one seems to know who wrote it. Sometimes it almost needs an explanation. Other times it explains itself. It is the story of someone who prayed:

> *He asked for strength that he might achieve.*
> *He was made weak that he might obey.*
> *He asked for power that he might do great things.*
> *He was given pain that he might do better things.*
> *He asked for wealth that he might be in comfort.*
> *He was made poor that he might be in sympathy.*
> *He asked for success that he might have the praise of men.*
> *He was given failure that he might feel the need of God.*
> *He asked for all things that he might enjoy life,*
> *He was given life that he might enjoy all things.*
> *He received nothing that he asked for . . .*
> *And yet all that he hoped for. His prayer was answered.*

How is it when we pray? God may not give the blessings we ask. Nevertheless he will fill our hearts to overflowing. Do you agree? Consider Jesus. He was not ashamed to ask. He asked God to take away the cup. Yet God gave him to drink from a sponge. God did not give what Jesus asked. Yet God gave all he hoped for. Gethsemane's prayer was wonderfully answered.

Blessed are they which do hunger and thirst after *righteousness*. What is "righteousness?" What is this for which we are supposed to thirst?

> *Jesus knew the blessedness of hungering and thirsting after righteousness.*

Jesus says it is being persecuted, reviled, all manner of evil against you. This is righteousness? Do you thirst for it? Like that cup of Jesus at Gethsemane, is this what you want filled up to the full?

What is righteousness? It is what put Jesus on the cross. He was righteous. And yet God made Jesus, says the scripture, "to be sin for us, who knew no sin; that we might be made the *righteousness* of God in him" (2 Cor. 5:21). Jesus himself *was* righteous. He hungered and thirsted after righteousness. But still, God made him to be sin for us. God did not give Jesus what he asked. Jesus pleaded, "take this cup from me." But God gave him the very dregs. God did not give what Jesus asked, yet Gethsemane's prayer was wonderfully answered.

"After this, Jesus knowing that all things were now accomplished that the scripture might be fulfilled, saith, I thirst." There on the cross, no cup. Only a sponge, pressed to our Lord's parched lips. Nevertheless Jesus drank of that and was filled. He was filled *with the knowing*. He knew he had done God's will. He knew all things were now accomplished. He knew the blessedness of hungering and thirsting after righteousness.

"I thirst." This word of Jesus is the beatitude crucified. And on the cross, in him, all righteousness is forever fulfilled. There is a prayer in which we Christians ask to be "filled with all the fullness of God." Ask God for that. Do not be ashamed to ask. God may not give you exactly what you ask. But what he gives will wonderfully fill your life. And even if it means carrying your cross after Christ, ask God for that. It will be your blessing. "Blessed are they which do hunger and thirst after righteousness."

—JOHN ALEXANDER MCELROY
From *Living with the Seven Words*

His Last Words
(Excerpt)

"I thirst! I thirst!" the Savior cried
 With burning lips before he died;
 A cooling draught he asked of those
 Who mocking looked upon his throes.

 Angelic hosts from heaven's height
 In sorrow gaze upon the sight;
 But yet the sky no water drips
 To cool the Savior's parched lips.

 A thousand fountains flowed that day,
 A river flowed not far away;
 But no one cup by friend or foe
 Was brought to mitigate his woe.

 He suffered thirst on Calvary's hill
 That he our thirsty hearts might fill,
 To open wide a fount of grace
 For all who seek the Saviour's face.

"O come!" we hear the spirit call—
 The invitation is to all:
"Ho, all ye souls athirst, come ye,
 And drink the living water free!"

—U<small>NKNOWN</small>

The Word of Suffering

"I thirst . . ."

—JOHN 19:28

"In my thirst they gave me vinegar to drink."
—ISAIAH 69:21

This is the shortest word from the Cross. In it is focused the physical pain endured by Christ our Redeemer. After the agony of spiritual suffering the pains of the body are uppermost. All human suffering is reflected in Christ's suffering. This was inevitable in the light of all that He had endured this far. The cry of personal need could not be stayed. He was the Son of Man and was not exempted from the pangs and pains common to humanity.

> *All human suffering is reflected in Christ's suffering.*

No one could endure all that He went through and fail to cry out in the crucible of suffering. Behind this cry were the dark and lonesome hours in Gethsemane when He accepted the bitter cup. There He was arrested and in the darkness of night hurried to the place of trial and judgment. During the waking hours of the morning He was mocked by the soldiers; and they inflicted upon Him those indignities of spitting, plucking the hair, striking Him on the cheek, dressing Him in kingly mockery, and bowing the knee in insult. Then He was led through the city to the place of Calvary. As He walked that solitary way He was faint; and another, Simon from Cyrene, assisted in the bearing of the Cross. Loss of sleep, the strain of the long night, the loss of blood, the cruel nails, and the tortured body. With a crown of thorns on His brow and bones out of joint, the gaping crowd mocked and jeered in their cry, "Away with him." All this found climax in the cry, "I thirst."

Hunger is a pain but thirst is greater. With thirst there is consciousness and clearness of mind in the midst of pain. In our Lord's experience, the hours were compressed with eternity. The scourging He endured left Him weak as He was "led as a lamb to the slaughter, and as a sheep before her shearers is dumb, so he opened not his mouth" (Isa. 53:7). Jesus was made perfect through suffering (Heb. 5:7–9) as the captain of our salvation. We do not have any stations of the cross as some others, but we do not forget that the sufferings of Christ were real and this cry was natural. Pain is not a delusion as some would teach in their denial of the reality of what our Lord went through for us. It is not scientific to deny suffering and it is no mark of spirituality to escape it. In the school of the Cross suffering is the highest class.

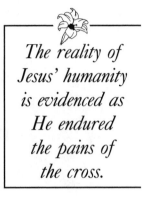

The reality of Jesus' humanity is evidenced as He endured the pains of the cross.

This word teaches that Jesus the Son of Man, God's Son, had taken a human body and our human nature. The human was joined to the divine nature. Here the reality of that humanity is evidenced as He endured the pains of the cross. He suffered in the flesh (I Peter 4:1). Suffering was no figment of the imagination or an illusion. The Christian faith accepts the reality of suffering because our Lord suffered and bled and died. What we call the Incarnation is simply the fact of God coming into life and taking to Himself our nature and living our life. Included in that are the limitations imposed by time and temporal boundaries, and includes suffering. As our representative man He sat where we sit.

> *The healing of His seamless dress*
> *Is by our beds of pain.*
> *We touch Him in life's throng and press*
> *And we are whole again.*

Think of the many who are confined to beds of sickness and suffering in our homes and hospitals. The cry arises to God from multitudes because of this afflicted state. In body and in mind there are those who agonize. Man cannot bring the remedy or the healing touch in every case. Only God knows why some are healed and others must continue to suffer. That is a mystery. The skill of medicine and science, the love of loved ones who pray, and beyond that the touch of the divine power which operates—by these God works His will in sovereign love. Not alone is there escape from suffering. Out of it have come some of the richest experiences known to man. Take the hymnbook and meditate on those hymns which speak of the Cross or tell of suffering. Then we begin to see that in the tapestry of like there is a weaving of dark as well as light colors permitted by God for our good.

George Matheson in his loss of sight wrote "O Love that will not let me go." Toplady, dying at thirty-eight years, a victim of tuberculosis, wasted in body, gave us "Rock of Ages, cleft for me." Francis Ridley Havergal in weakness composed "Take my life and let it be, Consecrated Lord to Thee." Who can estimate the power and influence of these hymns as well as countless others. Their healing ministry continues to bless the lives of multitudes.

> *Out of suffering have come some of the richest experiences known to man.*

If God does not heal in every case of suffering there is the opportunity to look at the Cross and hear this Sufferer's cry, "I thirst." In it God is suffering for us and with us. God did not exempt His only begotten Son from that experience. He endured the bloody seat and the agony of the tree.

This may be surprising, but think of what preceded. We must distinguish between two offerings of drink at the Crucifixion. At the beginning of the ordeal it was the custom for the soldiers to offer a victim some spiced wine. They knew the pains their victims had to bear, and to deaden the cries they offered this drug. Bringing it on a sponge they gave it to the victim to drink so that the drugged wine might induce stupefaction. Thus insensibility would result, the pains would be lessened, and the victim lose consciousness until he expired slowly.

All this was common to the crucified victims but not to Jesus. When He was offered that drink at the beginning He refused the intoxicating wine. He would not dull His senses or deaden the pain. This offer of anodyne or soporific was the only kindness in the midst of the callous and brutal task of the soldiers. Jesus refused the proffered drug. This proves and demonstrates the reality of his humanity. He did not die drugged, but with senses clear and mind alert. He would speak those seven words of love so that the world would know He was not a victim but the victor over death.

In this light we see that the cry was unnatural as far as man was concerned. Now He will request some drink to moisten His lips *after* suffering and enduring to the end. Then a soldier ran with a reed of hyssop filled with sour vinegar, not for Jesus to drink but to moisten His lips. On this sponge the sharp vinegar cooled the fever of the tongue which was parched in the agony of crucifixion. Jesus received this favor from one who was an instrument of wrong to Him.

> *The cry, "I thirst" truly came out of Jesus' physical sufferings.*

One day during His ministry Jesus asked a woman by a well to give Him a drink. She was an outcast of society in that place. Now He asks this same favor from a Roman soldier equally out of line with divine love. When the other soldiers saw Jesus' agony and heard His cry of dereliction, they did not run to Him, except this one. He gave the drink to Jesus while the others said, "Let be; let us see whether Elias will come to save him," confusing the Aramaic "Eloi" with "Elias," when Jesus cried, "My God." Did the soldier who assisted Jesus have a spark of kindness in him or had something touched his heart when Jesus cried out?

This is the only adequate explanation for the cry, "I thirst." Truly it came out of Jesus' physical sufferings, but it was not so confined. Was He implying something else in reference to His ministry and redemptive work? He who began His ministry hungry in the area of temptation now ends His ministry thirsting. He who was known as the Bread of Life and was hungry, now is seen as the Water of Life and is thirsty. The woman at the well found the water of life and now a Roman soldier is by the well of salvation.

"After this, Jesus knowing that all things were now accomplished, that the scripture might be fulfilled, saith, I thirst" (v. 28). This points to the completion of the work of redeeming sinful man. Before the final cry of triumph which was to follow, Jesus spoke of His thirst in the light of the fulfillment of scripture. The writer and evangelist knew the prophecy concerning Messiah's sufferings. He saw in these words the fulfillment of Psalm 59:21; but we should not omit the words of Psalm 22:15 which describe the thirst of Jesus: "My strength is dried up like a potsherd; and my tongue cleaveth to my jaws; and thou hast brought me into the dust of death."

Here Jesus is dying not as a weak, suffering mortal, but as God, as captain of our salvation, in complete charge of the situation, even when apparently helpless. The active obedience and the passive surrender to this death were at an end, in that He had suffered enough. He prepared Himself to die. He now would terminate the agony by His own action.

In Jesus' cry of thirst is gathered up all the cries of man's quest and desire for salvation.

The words concerning "I thirst" (Psa. 22:15) were spoken in order that scripture might be fulfilled. This reference brings to mind the truth of prophecy relative to the death of our Lord. To some moderns this sounds mechanical that Jesus spoke in order to fulfill prophecy. However we must do justice to the conception of John who reported the facts as historical. Then in the case of our Lord's personality as unique we must reckon with the natural prompting for relief of that frightful thirst that parched His lips, and the *divine consciousness* of the stage He had reached in the transaction of redemption.

> *In every pang that rends the heart,*
> *The Man of Sorrows hath a part,*
> *Finds confirmation here.*

It is here that we see how Jesus had finished the work of redemption by His sufferings. They were vicarious in that they were borne for others. They were divine in that God was in Christ suffering. All the pathos of this pain He endured is now summed up in His cry of thirst. This is more than the natural cry of a man as a victim; it is the voice of God crying out as proof of the truth that "He tasted death for every man" (Heb. 2:9).

In the cry of thirst is gathered up all the cries of man's quest and desire for salvation. Jesus in supra-natural power could see the crowd not alone as the group crucifying Him but also as those who would cry out for salvation. He had come for that end. All His sufferings are ended now. He can proclaim His victory and commit His soul to God in death and resurrection. Only now He sees the thirsty souls of men as they seek and search for the ultimate satisfactions of life and fail to find. All the wells of the world are broken cisterns and mock the seeker in that quest. Here at the Cross the wells of salvation are opened.

From the cry on the Cross Jesus must have recalled that great day of the feast in Jerusalem when He cried, "If any man thirst, let him come unto me and drink. He that believeth on me, as the scripture hath said, out of him shall flow rivers of living water. But this spake he of the Spirit, which they that believe on him should receive: for the Holy Spirit was not yet . . ." (John 7:37–39). To drink is the effect of faith or coming to Christ personally. In the Feast of Tabernacles and Dedication, Jesus proclaimed Himself as the Water of Life. Now in the Cross as He thirsts physically He also confirms that He is the Water of Life. The blessing is linked with the coming of the Spirit and His glorification. Only through suffering and death as the prelude to resurrection and ascension glory could this be. It is through union with the living Christ that the believer receives the blessings purchased through the atoning death.

> *Jesus' death was a sacrifice for others and an offering to satisfy eternal justice.*

Jesus knew suffering; and this greatest of all sufferings came at the end of life as He faced death itself. His death was a sacrifice for others and an offering to satisfy eternal justice. In His sufferings we see the penal woes that expiated human guilt. It was necessary for Him to endure these pains in order that as Captain of our salvation He might be perfected and touched with the feeling of our infirmities. It was not alone something which He endured but that which He did; hence its efficacy and merit on our behalf. Thus He thirsts still for our love and life in devotion. Well might our answer be:

> *I came to Jesus, and I drank*
> *Of that life-giving stream.*
> *My thirst was quenched, My soul revived,*
> *And now I live in Him.*

> —RALPH G. TURNBULL
> From *The Seven Words from the Cross*

RALPH G. TURNBULL—The Reverend Ralph G. Turnbull was born in Scotland and joined the First Presbyterian Church of Seattle, Washington in 1954 after attending Pittsburg Seminary. He is the editor of *Proclaiming the New Testament,* and the author of *A History of Preaching.* Dr. Turnbull, an avid follower of C. H. Spurgeon, said, "When the call came to leave business for the business of life in the ministry of the gospel, Spurgeon's sermons were gathered and read. Living with this treasure of truth for many years, a taste for Biblical truth was cultivated."

Jesus Speaks for the Needy

The tragedy on Calvary was near an end. The heat of the day and the closeness of death had taken the sharp edge of enthusiasm from those

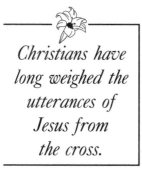

Christians have long weighed the utterances of Jesus from the cross.

who were using the occasion to heap a final ridicule upon Christ. The crowd was silent.

The parched lips of the Master moved. Speech was difficult. "I thirst!" he whispered.

We understand such a cry! There have been times when we too have been hot and thirsty. We have wanted a cool drink after a period of physical testing which could not be compared to that which Jesus experienced.

The Master was pleading for a friendly hand to perform a desperately needed service. It was a soldier, evidently, who responded. A vessel of vinegar had been brought from the city. He dipped a sponge into a dish, set the sponge on a stick, and lifted it to the mouth of Jesus. For whatever it was worth, that kindness was extended to him. His lips at least were moistened.

Christians have weighed each of the seven recorded utterances of Jesus from the cross. Keys to eternal truth have been suggested by the words which he spoke. The obvious physical need of the Master which brought forth the Fifth Word has often led students of the Gospels to dispose of it as merely an added clue to the depth of suffering which he endured.

But the Cross gives hints of spiritual certainty which help to satisfy the needs of men in every generation. It etches the longings and hopes of all mankind, as well as the faith by which each of us may live. That is the mission of the Fifth Word. "I thirst!" is a dramatic picture of something real, something tragic, which is always happening in the world.

Francis of Assisi came to an hour when the events which occurred on Calvary were the supreme concern of his life. He listened intently to the words which were spoken by the Christ. From then on he began to hear a sad, lonely murmur of need in every street and byway. "I thirst!" came from the lips of little children who were hungry and homeless. "I thirst!" came from the outcasts and the unwanted in a hundred Italian villages. The voice of Jesus asking for something to drink was a summons to Francis to quicken his hearing to the endless cries of people for help.

Before he understood what the Cross demanded of him, Francis had passed by beggars and cripples without giving them a second glance. He enjoyed the pleasures of daily living too much to be aware of its tragedy. That attitude was changed when he recaptured the events of the first Good Friday. A steady gaze at the crucified Christ transformed his manner of living. As he walked the busy streets or loitered in the noisy market place, he heard the cry of pitiful men and women and children on every hand.

"I thirst!" is a dramatic picture of something real, something tragic, which is always happening in the world.

Unless we are satisfied to allow the Cross to remain merely a pageant, the same experience will be repeated in our daily lives. When we think only of ourselves, the suffering of Jesus remains a drama which has no meaning. It never pierces the armor which we carry to protect privilege and possessions against Christ's insistent demand that every attitude and outlook be refined. Those of us who are determined to make Jesus the Lord and Master of our lives test all we say and all we do by the Cross. We will hear Jesus' cry "I thirst" in every pitiful entreaty which comes from needy humanity.

—G. ERNEST THOMAS
From *Daily Meditations on the Seven Last Words*

CHAPTER NINE

The Death

The Death

LUKE 23:46

⁴⁶And when Jesus had cried out with a loud voice, He said, "Father, 'into Your hands I commit My spirit.' " Having said this, He breathed His last.

This Must Be the Lamb

On a gray April morning as a chilling wind blew,
A thousand dark promises were about to come true.
As Satan stood trembling, knowing now he had lost,
As the Lamb took His first step on the way to the cross.

This must be the Lamb,
The fulfillment of all God had spoken.
This must be the Lamb,
Not a single bone will be broken.
Like a sheep to the slaughter,
So silently still,
This must be the Lamb.

They mocked His true calling and laughed at His fate,
So glad to see the Gentle One consumed by their hate.
Unaware of the wind and the darkening sky,
So blind to the fact that it was God limping by.

This must be the Lamb,
The fulfillment of all God had spoken.

This must be the Lamb,
Not a single bone will be broken.
Like a sheep to the slaughter,
So silently still,
This must be the Lamb.

The poor women weeping at what seemed a great loss,
Trembling in fear there at the foot of the cross.
Tormented by memories that came like a flood,
Unaware that their pardon must be bought by His blood.

This must be the Lamb,
The fulfillment of all God had spoken.
This must be the Lamb,
Not a single bone will be broken.
Like a sheep to the slaughter,
So silently still,
This must be the Lamb.

—MICHAEL CARD
From *Immanuel: Reflections
on the Life of Christ*

The Lion, the Witch, and the Wardrobe
(Excerpt)

A great crowd of people were standing all round the Stone Table and though the moon was shining many of them carried torches which burned with evil-looking red flames and black smoke. But such people! Ogres with monstrous teeth, and wolves, and bull-headed men; spirits of evil trees and poisonous plants; and other creatures whom I won't describe because if I did the grown-ups would probably not let you read this book—Cruels and Hags and Incubuses, Wraiths, Horrors, Efreets,

CARVING BY SUZANNE YOUNG
PHOTO BY SOBEIRA SALDIVAR-ZALENSKI

St. Hugo of the Hills Catholic Church
Bloomfield Hills, MI

STATIONS OF THE CROSS
Station 2 – Christ is Given the Cross
Unglazed porcelain carving

CARVING BY SUZANNE YOUNG
PHOTO BY SOBEIRA SALDIVAR-ZALENSKI

St. Hugo of the Hills Catholic Church
Bloomfield Hills, MI

STATIONS OF THE CROSS
Station 3 – Christ Falls for the First Time
Unglazed porcelain carving

CARVING BY SUZANNE YOUNG
PHOTO BY SOBEIRA SALDIVAR-ZALENSKI

St. Hugo of the Hills Catholic Church
Bloomfield Hills, MI

STATIONS OF THE CROSS

Station 5 – Simon of Cyrene is Forced to Help Christ Carry the Cross

Unglazed porcelain carving

CARVING BY SUZANNE YOUNG
PHOTO BY SOBEIRA SALDIVAR-ZALENSKI

St. Hugo of the Hills Catholic Church
Bloomfield Hills, MI

STATIONS OF THE CROSS
Station 7 - Christ Falls for the Second Time
Unglazed porcelain carving

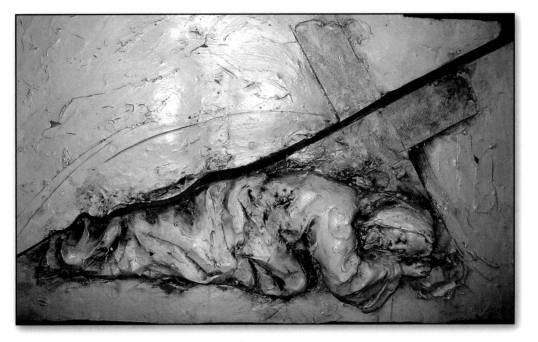

CARVING BY SUZANNE YOUNG
PHOTO BY SOBEIRA SALDIVAR-ZALENSKI

St. Hugo of the Hills Catholic Church
Bloomfield Hills, MI

STATIONS OF THE CROSS
Station 9 – Christ Falls for the Third Time
Unglazed porcelain carving

CARVING BY SUZANNE YOUNG
PHOTO BY SOBEIRA SALDIVAR-ZALENSKI

St. Hugo of the Hills Catholic Church
Bloomfield Hills, MI

STATIONS OF THE CROSS

Station 12 – Christ Dies on the Cross

Unglazed porcelain carving

SALVADOR DALI (1904-1989)   *The St. Mungo Museum of Religious Life and Art, Glasgow*

CHRIST OF ST. JOHN OF THE CROSS

REMBRANDT VAN RIJN (1606-1669)

CHRIST CRUCIFIED
BETWEEN THE TWO THIEVES

(The Three Crosses)

Drypoint and engraving, fourth state (38.5 x 45.0 cm)

Sprites, Orknies, Wooses, and Ettins. In fact here were all those who were on the Witch's side and whom the Wolf had summoned at her command. And right in the middle, standing by the Table, was the Witch herself.

A howl and a gibber of dismay went up from the creatures when they first saw the great Lion pacing towards them, and for a moment the Witch herself seemed to be struck with fear. Then she recovered herself and gave a wild, fierce laugh.

"The fool!" she cried. "The fool has come. Bind him fast."

Lucy and Susan held their breaths waiting for Aslan's roar and his spring upon his enemies. But it never came. Four hags, grinning and leering, yet also (at first) hanging back and half afraid of what they had to do, had approached him. "Bind him, I say!" repeated the White Witch. The hags made a dart at him and shrieked with triumph when they found that he made no resistance at all. Then others—evil dwarfs and apes— rushed in to help them and between them they rolled the huge Lion round on his back and tied all his four paws together, shouting and cheering as if they had done something brave, though, had the Lion chose, one of those paws could have been the death of them all. But he made no noise, even when the enemies, straining and tugging, pulled the cords so tight that they cut into his flesh. Then they begun to drag him towards the Stone Table.

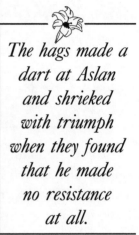

The hags made a dart at Aslan and shrieked with triumph when they found that he made no resistance at all.

"Stop!" said the Witch. "Let him first be shaved."

Another roar of mean laughter went up from her followers as an ogre with a pair of shears came forward and squatted down by Aslan's head. Snip-snip-snip went the shears and masses of curling gold began to fall to the ground. Then the ogre stood back and the children, watching from their hiding-place, could see the face of Aslan looking all small and different without its mane. The enemies also saw the difference.

"Why, he's only a great cat after all!" cried one.

"Is *that* what we were afraid of?" said another.

And they surged round Aslan jeering at him, saying things like "Puss, Puss! Poor Pussy," and "How many mice have you caught to-day, Cat?" and "Would you like a saucer of milk, Pussums?"

"Oh how *can* they?" said Lucy, tears streaming down her cheeks. "The brutes, the brutes!" for now that the first shock was over the shorn face of Aslan looked to her braver, and more beautiful, and more patient than ever.

"Muzzle him!" said the Witch. And even now, as they worked about his face putting on the muzzle, one bite from his jaws would have cost two or three of them their hands. But he never moved. And this seemed to enrage all that rabble. Everyone was at him now. Those who had been afraid to come near him even after he was bound began to find their courage, and for a few minutes the two girls could not even see him—so thickly was he surrounded by the whole crowd of creatures kicking him, hitting him, spitting on him, jeering at him.

> *When once Aslan had been tied on the flat stone, a hush fell on the crowd.*

At last the rabble had had enough of this. They began to drag the bound and muzzled Lion to the Stone Table, some pulling and some pushing. He was so huge that even when they got him there it took all their efforts to hoist him onto the surface of it. Then there was more tying and tightening of the cords.

"The cowards! The cowards!" sobbed Susan. "Are they *still* afraid of him, even now?"

When once Aslan had been tied (and tied so that he was really a mass of cords) on the flat stone, a hush fell on the crowd. Four Hags, holding four torches, stood at the corners of the Table. The Witch bared her arms as she had bared them the previous night when it had been Edmund instead of Aslan. Then she began to whet her knife. It looked to the children, when the gleam of the torchlight fell on it, as if the knife were made of stone not of steel and it was of a strange and evil shape.

At last she drew near. She stood by Aslan's head. Her face was working and twitching with passion, but his looked up at the sky, still quiet, neither angry nor afraid, but a little sad. Then, just before she gave the blow, she stooped down and said in a quivering voice, "And now, who has won? Fool, did you think that by all this you would save the human traitor? Now I will kill you instead of him as our pact was and so the Deep Magic will be appeased. But when you are dead what will prevent me from killing him as well? And who will take him out of my hand *then*? Understand that you have given me Narnia forever, you have lost your own life and you have not saved his. In that knowledge, despair and die."

The children did not see the actual moment of the killing. They couldn't bear to look and had covered their eyes.

While the two girls still crouched in the bushes with their hands over their faces, they heard the voice of the Witch calling out.

"Now! Follow me all and we will set about what remains of this war! It will not take us long to crush the human vermin and the traitors now that the great Fool, the great Cat, lies dead."

—C. S. Lewis

When I Survey the Wondrous Cross

When I survey the wondrous cross
On which the Prince of glory died,
My richest gain I count but loss,
And pour contempt on all my pride.
Forbid it, Lord, that I should boast,
Save in the death of Christ my God!
All the vain things that charm me most,
I sacrifice them to His blood.
See from His head, His hands, His feet,
Sorrow and love flow mingled down!
Did e'er such love and sorrow meet,
Or thorns compose so rich a crown?

His dying crimson, like a robe,
Spreads o'er His body on the tree;
Then I am dead to all the globe,
And all the globe is dead to me.
Were the whole realm of nature mine,
That were a present far too small:
Love so amazing, so divine,
Demands my soul, my life, my all.

[The last verse is by an unknown author]
To Christ, Who won for sinners grace
By bitter grief and anguish sore,
Be praise from all the ransomed race
Forever and forevermore.

—ISAAC WATTS

What We Behold on the Cross

"As they were looking on, so we too gaze on his wounds as he hangs. We see his blood as he dies. We see the price offered by the redeemer, touch the scars of his resurrection. He bows his head, as if to kiss you.

> *We see the price offered by the redeemer, touch the scars of his resurrection.*

His heart is made bare open, as it were, in love to you. His arms are extended that he may embrace you. His whole body is displayed for your redemption. Ponder how great these things are. Let all this be rightly weighed in your mind: as he was once fixed to the cross in every part of his body for you, so he may now be fixed in every part of your soul." [GMI 248]

—AUGUSTINE OF HIPPO

AUGUSTINE OF HIPPO (A.D. 354–430)—Augustine of Hippo was born in Tagaste, Algiers, which was then a part of Roman Africa. His parents, Patricius and Monica, had high hopes for their children, but could not afford to pursue their educations. With the help of a wealthy friend, Augustine was sent to the university in Madaura. In 393, Augustine was asked to preach in place of the Bishop of Hippo, and being so good at it, assumed the responsibilities of the bishop when he died two years later. His services can only be described as "standing room only" and he reportedly sermonized with such imagination, no one minded standing for up to two hours on a Sunday.

Good Friday, 1613. Riding Westward

Let man's soul be a sphere, and then, in this,
The intelligence that moves, devotion is,
And as the other Spheres, by being grown
Subject in a year their natural form obey:
Pleasure or business, so, our souls admit
For their first mover, and are whirl'd by it.
Hence, is't, that I am carried towards the west
This day, when my soul's form bends toward the east
There I should see a sun, by rising set,
And by that setting endless day beget;
But that Christ on this cross, did rise and fall,
Sin had eternally benighted all.
Yet dare I almost be glad, I do not see
That spectacle of too much weight for me.
Who sees God's face, that is self life, must die;
What a death were it then to see God die?
It made his own lieutenant, Nature, shrink,
It made his footstool crack, and the sun wink.
Could I behold those hands which span the poles,
And turn all spheres at once, pierced with those holes?
Could I behold that endless height which is
Zenith to us, and our Antipodes,

Humbled below us? or that blood which is
The seat of all our souls, if not of his,
Made dirt of dust, or that flesh which was worn
By God, for his apparel, ragg'd and torn?
If on these things I durst not look, durst I
Upon his miserable mother cast mine eye,
Who was God's partner here, and furnished thus
Half of that sacrifice, which ransomed us?
Though these things, as I ride, be from mine eye,
They are present yet to my memory,
For that looks towards them; and thou look'st towards me,
I turn my back to thee, but to receive
Corrections, till thy mercies bid thee leave.
O think me worth thine anger, punish me,
Burn off my rusts, and my deformity,
Restore thine image, so much, by thy grace,
That thou may'st know me, and I'll turn my face.

—JOHN DONNE
From *The Lion Christian*
Poetry Collection

Quote

". . . There is but One Who Dyed salvically for us, and able to say unto Death, 'Hitherto shalt thou go, and no farther;' only one enlivening Death, which makes Gardens of Graves, and that which was sowed in Corruption to arise and flourish in Glory: when Death it self shall dye, and living shall have no Period, when the damned shall mourn at the funeral of Death, when Life not Death shall be the wages of sin, when the second Death shall prove a miserable Life, and destruction shall be courted."

—SIR THOMAS BROWN

Pange, lingua

Sing, my tongue, the glorious battle,
Sing the ending of the fray.
Now alone the cross, the trophy,
Sound the loud triumphant lay;
Tell how Christ, the world's redeemer,
As a victim won the day.

—CHRISTUS VICTOR

Immanuel: Reflections on the Life of Christ
(Excerpt)

It was John the Baptist who first recognized Jesus as the "Lamb of God." "Behold! The Lamb of God who takes away the sin of the world!" he shouted as Jesus approached. The sacrificial "seal of approval" had already been placed on Jesus.

The Old Testament says a lot about sacrificial lambs. The children of Israel sacrificed them and painted the doorposts of their houses in Egypt with the blood so the angel of death would "Passover" their houses. In the New Testament Jesus is our Passover Lamb. We mark the doorposts of our hearts, as it were, with His blood so the angel that is the second death will "Passover" us.

The children of Israel sacrificed lambs and painted the doorposts of their houses in Egypt with the blood.

One of the details of the offering of the Passover lamb was that none of its bones were to be broken. It was permitted to pull the carcass apart at the joint, but the bones were to be kept intact. When Jesus is crucified the apostle John is moved by the fact that His bones were kept from being broken. The Jews did not want the bodies of the three crucified men left on the crosses during their Passover. They were afraid it might dampen the celebration! They went to Pilate with an almost unbelievably gruesome request. Because the prisoners had to be dead before they were taken down, and there was a good chance that all three were still alive, (crucifixion usually took days to kill a victim), the priests asked that the legs of the three crucified men be broken so that their deaths might be hurried along.

> *Since Jesus was already dead, there was no need for the soldiers to break His legs, as was the custom to bring about a more immediate death.*

The Romans used a heavy wooden mallet to break the two lower leg bones, causing the full weight of the body to be brought to bear on the chest, causing a quicker death by suffocation. As horrible a death as crucifixion was, it is hard to think of how it might have been made worse. But the breaking of the legs, though bringing about a more immediate death, must have been excruciating. (The Latin root for *excruciating* is the word for *cross*.)

The two thieves on either side of Jesus were apparently still alive. Like most other victims of crucifixion, they would probably have lasted for days. The soldiers broke the legs of both men. When they came to Jesus, however, they discovered that He was already dead. He had "dismissed" His spirit with the words of Psalm 31:5, "Into your hands I commit my spirit." (He had earlier quoted Psalm 22:1.) Since He was already dead, there was no need for the soldiers to break His legs. The prophecy of Psalm 34:20, "He protects all His bones, not one of them will be broken," was perfectly fulfilled. To make sure Jesus was dead, the soldiers pierced His side with a spear, causing blood and water from the broken sack around His heart to flow.

Three years earlier in that uncluttered countryside, when John had shouted across the Jordan, "Behold, the Lamb of God," who would have ever thought it would mean this?

—MICHAEL CARD

The Killing

That was the day they killed the Son of God
On a squat hill-top by Jerusalem.
Zion was bare, her children from their maze
Sucked by the demon curiosity
Clean through the gates. The very halt and blind
Had somehow got themselves up to the hill.

After the ceremonial preparation,
The scourging, nailing, nailing against the wood,
Erection of the main-trees with their burden,
While from the hill rose an orchestral wailing,
They were there at last, high up in the soft spring day.
We watched the writhings, heard the moanings, saw
The three heads turning on their separate axles
Like broken wheels left spinning. Round *his* head
Was loosely bound a crown of plaited thorn
That hurt at random, stinging temple and brow
As the pain swung into its envious circle.
In front the wreath was gathered in a knot
That as he gazed looked like the last stump left
Of a death-wounded deer's great antlers. Some
Who came to stare grew silent as they looked,
Indignant or sorry. But the hardened old
And the hard-hearted young, although at odds
From the first morning, cursed him with one curse,
Having prayed for a Rabbi or an armed Messiah
And found the Son of God. What use to them
Was a God or a Son of God? Of what avail
For purposes such as theirs? Beside the cross-foot,
Alone, four women stood and did not move

All day. The sun revolved, the shadow wheeled,
The evening fell. His head lay on his breast,
But in his breast they watched his heart move on
By itself alone, accomplishing its journey.
Their taunts grew louder, sharpened by the knowledge
That he was walking in the park of death,
Far from their rage. Yet all grew stale at last,
Spite, curiosity, envy, hate itself.
They waited only for death and death was slow
And came so quietly they scarce should mark it.
They were angry then with death and death's deceit.

I was a stranger, could not read these people
Or this outlandish deity. Did a God
Indeed in dying cross my life that day
By chance, he on his road and I on mine?

—EDWIN MUIR
From *The Gospels in
Our Image*

Palm Sunday: Good Friday

It was but now their sounding clamours sung,
'Blessed is he that comes from the Most High',
And all the mountains with 'Hosanna' rung,
And now, 'Away with him, away,' they cry,
And nothing can be heard but 'Crucify!'
    It was but now the crown itself they save,
    And golden name of King unto him gave,
And now no King but only Caesar they will have.

It was but now they gathered blooming May,
And of his arms disrobed the branching tree,
To strew with boughs and blossoms all thy way,
And now, the branchless trunk a cross for thee,
And May, dismayed, thy coronet must be:
   It was but now they were so kind to throw
   Their own best garments where thy feet should go,
And now, thyself they strip, and bleeding wounds they show.

See where the author of all life is dying.
O fearful day! He dead, what hope of living?
See where the hopes of all our lives are buying.
O cheerful day! They bought, what fear of grieving?
Love love for hate, and death for life is giving:
   Lo, how his arms are stretched abroad to grace thee,
   And, as, they open stand, call to embrace thee.
Why stay'st thou then my soul: O fly, fly thither haste thee.

—GILES FLETCHER THE YOUNGER
From *The Lion Christian Poetry Collection*

> **GILES FLETCHER THE YOUNGER** (1585–1623)—Giles Fletcher had strong family ties to poetic talent. His father, Giles Fletcher the elder, was an English writer and diplomat, while his brother, Phineas, was a noted poet. He was educated at Trinity College, Cambridge, and served as a reader in Greek until 1618. He became the rector at Alderton, Suffolk in 1619. Fletcher's most famous poem is *Christ's Victory and Triumph*.

On the Significance of the Son of God

"Of man's first disobedience, and the fruit
   Of that forbidden tree, whose mortal taste
   Brought death into the world, and all our woe,

With loss of Eden, till one great Man
Restore us, and regain that blissful seat . . ."

—JOHN MILTON
From *Paradise Lost*

Reminder
(Mark 15:21–32)

My key-ring keeps the design of redemption
pendant from my ignition and,
when I'm walking, repeats the sound
of nails noisily in my pocket.

The same bloodsoaked timbers that sighed
the worst of deaths, pinning a spreadeagled
Christ to the sky, are used in my town
for life-raft Fonts and picnic Tables.

Death, not Christ, changed the meaning when Christ
and cross were joined. Murder was a catalyst
for mercy. And so my metal ring
sings its small hymn in cadence with my heart.

—EUGENE H. PETERSON
From *A Widening Light:*
Poems of the Incarnation

EUGENE H. PETERSON—Eugene H. Peterson is known for his acclaimed translation of the New Testament, *The Message.* Before his retirement, he was a Theology professor at Regent College in Vancouver, B.C., as well as the founding pastor of Christ Our King Presbyterian Church in Bel Air, Maryland. He is also a member of the editorial council of *Theology Today.*

Immanuel: Reflections on the Life of Christ
(Excerpt)

It was an unusually warm day for early February. I had come into our small town to do a few errands, and especially to get a little gift for my wife. At the last minute, our friend Dan had given us tickets for a play, so I was trying to arrange a special evening as I could on such short notice. I finally decided on a corsage, the kind boys used to give girls on prom night. That's what I wanted our date to feel like, prom night.

Our town, Franklin, was the scene of one of the bloodiest battles of the Civil War. Since the state did not have the funds to buy property on the battlefield, there is no state park here to commemorate the battle as there are for many other battles that were much smaller in scale. All that's here is a museum called "The Carter

Almost seven thousand men died in a battle that lasted only five hours.

House," a small house that actually survived being located in the center of the battle. The Carter House still stands today, on Columbia Pike, a despairingly small monument to a very bloody battle.

Almost seven thousand men died in the immediate vicinity of that house in a battle that lasted only five hours. The Federal troops used up one hundred wagon loads of ammunition in that short time. I've read accounts of bodies being stacked six and seven deep for more than a mile along Columbia Pike. Even the most hardened soldiers said that after the battle that they had never seen anything like it.

The flower shop that had my corsage is located next door to the Carter House. When I placed my order the lady at the desk said that it would be fifteen or twenty minutes before my flowers would be ready. It was such a beautiful day outside I decided to go into the yard of the shop and wait.

Two of the original outbuildings are still standing beside the Carter

House. They are peppered with bullet holes on the sides of the buildings that faced the battle. On the opposite sides are the exit holes. I walked over to one of the small reddish buildings and examined the evidence of the battle. The main earth works (trenches dug by the Federal troops where the center of the battle was fought) passed directly through what is now the side yard of the flower shop. The fiercest part of the battle had raged right where I was standing. You can still make out a slight indentation in the ground. That shallow dip in the earth is all that is left. Hundreds of bodies were simply left in these trenches when they were filled in, a mass burial.

> *How could this happen? How could such a mountain of pain and suffering ever be covered up, erased, and all but forgotten?*

As I stood beside the wall of the mass structure, looking at what little physical evidence of the battle was left, I was struck by the most profound realization of what had really happened there. The horror and the blood. The screams of the wounded and dying. Seven thousand of them! I could almost see the bodies strewn there, hear the cries for water, the sounds of wounded men and horses. The loss of so many young lives. So many families destroyed. The bitterness of such defeat still hangs on in some pockets of the South.

The scars of the battle have all but been erased. Flowers grow where the lines once were. One of the workers showed me human teeth that had just surfaced the day before after a long rain.

"It happens all the time," he said nonchalantly.

Across the street is a pizza place and some small shops. High school kids gather and eat pizza where hundreds of men brutally lost their lives. I kept asking myself, *How could this happen? How could such a mountain of pain and suffering ever be covered up, erased, and all but forgotten? How could men build flower shops and pizza stands on such hallowed ground?*

As I was driving home, still somewhat dazed and with Susan's corsage now safely in tow, a second, no less powerful realization struck me. I had been so awestruck in that back yard that was once a battlefield, and yet everyday I stand before a token of suffering, which overshadows that forgotten battle as a mountain overshadows a grain of sand. It is the cross, of course.

There must have been a time in my life when I was awestruck by the cross in the same way I was that day beside the flower shop. But, God forgive me, I can't remember when it was.

Perhaps we do not grasp the magnitude of the cross because we cannot possibly hope to grasp it. We dwell on the physical agony of Jesus, the nails and the thorns, but they make up only the most minute portion of His suffering. There are people alive today that have suffered such pain, and even more. What cannot be grasped by any living soul is the spiritual and emotional agony of Jesus. It is impossible.

The cross was the only moment in all eternity when Jesus was separated from the Father. They had always been One. But now, quite unimaginably, They were separated by our sin.

Jesus cried out, "Why have You forsaken Me?" precisely because God did forsake Him there. As the pure and spotless Lamb of God became sin for you and me, the Father had to look away, for the Bible tells us that His eyes are too holy to look upon sin. On the cross, for the only time in eternity, the Father took His eyes off of the Son as the Son's tear-filled eyes looked for the Father.

> *As the pure and spotless Lamb of God became sin for you and me, the Father had to look away, for the Bible tells us that His eyes are too holy to look upon sin.*

When the creeds say that Jesus descended into hell, that is what they mean. Hell is separation from God, separation from everything that is good, that is life and light. Hell is the price to pay for sin. And so that is what Jesus paid. The darkness that covered Him there on Golgotha wasn't an atmospheric phenomenon as much as it was a spiritual reality. In one sense the darkness must have radiated from Jesus, not around Him. For if darkness is the visible manifestation of sin, and Jesus became sin on the cross for you and me, then the darkness that covered Him there was as much from Him as around Him. He who was the Light became darkness on the cross. Jesus, who was the Life, not only became dead on the cross, but became in some sense Death itself.

In some indescribable way, the death of one man can be more significant, more revoking, than the death of a thousand. At the battle of Franklin the youngest son of the Carters, a boy named Todd, was killed almost in his own front yard, trying to make it home. Today he is spoken of and written about more than the other 6,999 men who also lost their lives that day. The poignant situation of his death somehow seems to eclipse the others.

Jesus' unspeakable death speaks more than a mountain of pain.

What about the Son of Man, whose unspeakable death speaks more than a mountain of pain? As we stand before the cross, we should feel as if we are standing upon a battlefield, the ground still wet with blood and pain. The screams, His cries of thirst, should still ring our ears. And what small part of that spiritual battle we can grasp, we must hold on to for all our lives because we were part of the reason for it. If we belong to Him, we are now a part of the battle itself and it is a part of us.

—MICHAEL CARD

Good Friday

O heart, be lifted up; O heart be gay,
Because the Light was lifted up today—
Was lifted on the Rood, but did not die,
To shine eternally for such as I.

O heart, rejoice with all your humble might
That God did kindle in the world this Light,
Which stretching on the Cross could not prevent
From shining with continuous intent.

Why weep, O heart, this day? Why grieve you so?
If all the glory of the Light had lost its glow
Would the sun shine or earth put on her best—
Her flower-entangled and embroidered vest?

Look up, O heart, and then, O heart, kneel down
In humble adoration: give no crown
Nor golden diadem to your fair Lord,
But offer love and beauty by your word . . .

The everlasting fire of love, O heart,
Has blazed in you and it will not depart.
Wherefore, O heart, exult and praises sing:
Lift up your voice and make the echoes ring . . .

O heart, rise up: O heart be lifted high,
Rejoice; for Light was slain today, yet did not die.

—ANONYMOUS
From *The Lion Christian
Poetry Collection*

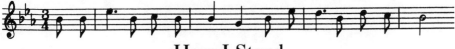

Here I Stand

*As I stand before the glory,
As I look upon the pain,
As I hear the sound of sorrow in the wind,
As the earth begins to tremble
Does it wonder?
What's the use of turning if Jesus'
Eyes are growing dim?*

*Enveloped in the darkness,
Surrounded by the night,
Could it be that life is death,*

And death is really life?
The only hope for meaning
The simple question why?
To be witness to the paradox
That God's about to die.

In this world of blind illusion,
Where the truth is called a lie,
As we stumble through the way of life,
How could You be my guide?
Do You really want my hopeless heart?
Do You long to love me so?
As I stand before the cross of love,
How can I answer no?

Amidst Your awful pain
I sense an overwhelming peace.
Beyond the nails and bonds
I see victorious release.
Unlike You I'm bound to time,
So I must live within the years.
I would long to come and be with You
And suffer through Your tears.

In this world of blind illusion,
Where the truth is called a lie,
As we stumble through the way of life,
How could you be my guide?
Do you really want my hopeless heart?
Do you long to love me so?
As I stand before the cross of love,
How can I answer no?

—MICHAEL CARD
From *Immanuel: Reflections*
on the Life of Christ

CHAPTER TEN

The Veil Split Asunder

The Veil Split Asunder

MATTHEW 27:51

> ⁵¹*Then, behold, the veil of the temple was torn in two from top to bottom; and the earth quaked, and the rocks were split.*

Pardon for the Greatest Sinner
(Excerpt)

"They who truly come to God for mercy, come as beggars, and not as creditors: they come for mere mercy, for sovereign grace, and not for any thing that is due.'

—JONATHAN EDWARDS

JONATHAN EDWARDS (1703–1758)—Jonathan Edwards was born in East Windsor, Connecticut and graduated from Yale College in 1716. After earning his Masters in Theology, he became the minister of Presbyterian Church in New York. He authored *Of Being, Diary, Resolutions, Miscellanies,* and *The Mind* before 1723. He married Sarah Pierpont, and then succeeded his grandfather, Solomon Stoddard, as the pastor of a church in Northampton, Massachusetts. He published *A Faithful Narrative of the Surprising Work of God*, which led to a revival in Northampton. Then, he published *A Treatise Concerning Religious Affections*. In 1750, he was dismissed as the pastor at Northampton and became a pastor and missionary to the Indians in Stockbridge, Massachusetts. It was at this time that Edwards wrote his greatest works, such as *Freedom of the Will* and *The Nature of True Virtue*. In 1758, Edwards became the President of the College of New Jersey, but tragically died a few months later from a smallpox inoculation.

The Rent Veil

*(A Sermon Delivered on Lord's-day
Morning, March 25th, 1888 at the Metropolitan
Tabernacle, Newington)*

The death of our Lord Jesus Christ was fitly surrounded by miracles; yet it is itself so much greater a wonder then all besides, that it as far exceeds them as the sun outshines the planets which surround it. It seems natural enough that the earth should quake, that tombs should be opened, and that the veil of the temple should be rent, when He who only hath immortality gives up the ghost. The more you think of the death of the Son of God, the more you will be amazed at it. As much as a miracle excels a common fact, so doth this wonder of wonders rise above all miracles of power. That the divine Lord, even though veiled in mortal flesh, should condescend to be subject to the power of death, so as to bow his head on the cross, and submit to be laid in the tomb, is among mysteries, the greatest. The death of Jesus is the marvel of time and eternity, which, as Aaron's rod swallowed up all the rest, takes up into itself all lesser marvels.

> *The rending of the veil of the temple is not a miracle to be lightly passed over.*

Yet the rending of the veil of the temple is not a miracle to be lightly passed over. It was made of "fine twined linen, with Cherubims of cunning work." This gives the idea of a substantial piece of fabric, a piece of lasting tapestry, which would have endured the severest strain. No human hands could have torn such a sacred covering; and it could not have been divided in the midst by any accidental cause; yet, strange to say, on the instant when the holy person of Jesus was rent by death, the great veil which concealed the holiest of all was "rent in twain from the top to the bottom." What did it mean? It meant much more than I can tell you now.

It is not fanciful to regard it as a solemn act of mourning on the part of the house of the Lord. In the East men express their sorrow by rending their garments; and the temple, when it beheld its Master die, seemed struck with horror, and rent its veil. Shocked at the sin of man, indignant at the murder of its Lord, in its sympathy with Him who is the true temple of God, the outward symbol tore its holy vestment from the top to the bottom. Did not the miracle also mean that from that hour the whole system of types, and shadows, and ceremonies had come to an end? The ordinances of an earthly priesthood were rent with that veil. In token of the death of ceremonial law, the soul of it quitted its sacred shrine, and left its bodily tabernacle as a dead thing. The legal dispensation is over. The rent of the veil seemed to say—"Henceforth God dwells no longer in the thick darkness of the Holy of Holies, and shines forth no longer from between the cherubim. The special enclosure is broken up, and there is no inner sanctuary for the earthly high priest to enter: typical atonements and sacrifices are at an end."

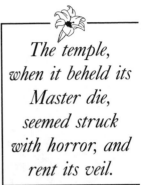

The temple, when it beheld its Master die, seemed struck with horror, and rent its veil.

According to the explanation given in our second text, the rending of the veil chiefly meant that the way into the holiest, which was not before made manifest, was now laid open to all believers. Once in the year the high priest lifted a corner of this veil with fear and trembling, and with blood and holy incense he passed into the immediate presence of Jehovah; but the tearing of the veil laid open the secret place. The rent from top to bottom gives ample space for all to enter who are called of God's grace, to approach the throne, and to commune with the Eternal One.

—C. H. Spurgeon

From Every Stormy Wind

From every stormy wind that blows,
From every swelling tide of woes,

There is a calm, a sure retreat;
'Tis found beneath the mercy seat.

There is a place where Jesus sheds
The oil of gladness on our heads;
A place than all besides more sweet;
It is the blood bought mercy seat.

There is a scene where spirits blend,
Where friend holds fellowship with friend;
Though sundered far, by faith they meet
Around one common mercy seat.

There, there, on eagles' wings we soar,
And time and sense seem all no more;
And heaven comes down, our souls to greet,
And glory crowns the mercy seat.

Oh, let my hand forget her skill,
My tongue be silent, cold, and still,
This bounding heart forget to beat,
If I forget the mercy seat!

—HUGH STOWELL
From *The Winter's Wreath, a Collection of
Original Contributions in Prose and Verse*

The Preeminent Person of Christ
(Excerpt)

The operating room of a hospital is a foreboding place—almost sacred.
The air is filtered, pure and clean. The walls and floors are immaculately

scrubbed. The instruments are sterilized. A sign hangs over the entrance—Unauthorized Persons: Keep Out.

The only people allowed in the operating room are trained physicians and select hospital personnel. But they, too, must be scrubbed and sterilized, wearing disposable hospital greens with protective masks and foot coverings.

In order for the operating room to fulfill the function for which it was made, it must be free from contamination. Even the smallest of germs can infiltrate and infect the very person who's there for help.

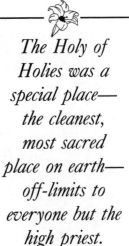

The Holy of Holies was a special place—the cleanest, most sacred place on earth—off-limits to everyone but the high priest.

The operating room is a special place, set apart for private usage for the most delicate of duties—the saving of human life. The Holy of Holies was a similar type of place. It was the cleanest, most sacred place on earth. It was off-limits to everyone except the high priest, and even he could only enter once a year, on the Day of Atonement. A large, tapestried veil separated the Holy of Holies from the rest of the temple. However, when Jesus died, that curtain was torn from top to bottom (Matt. 27:51). The veil had warned, "Keep out!" but the tearing of the veil tacitly announced, "Come in!" Since the blood of Christ cleansed us from all of sin's contamination, we are now free—not only to enter, but to enter with confidence.

—CHARLES SWINDOLL

CHARLES SWINDOLL—Charles Swindoll is Chancellor of Dallas Theological Seminary, chairman of *Insight for Living*, and Senior Pastor of Stonebriar Community Church in Frisco, Texas. He has authored more than twenty-five best-selling books, including *Joseph, Esther, David, Elijah, Grace Awakening* and *Laugh Again*. His practical application of the Bible to everyday living makes God's truths a reality to hurting people. He and his wife, Cynthia, have four children and ten grandchildren.

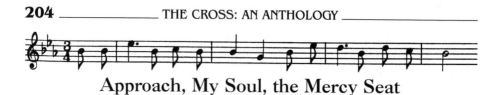

Approach, My Soul, the Mercy Seat

Approach, my soul, the mercy seat,
Where Jesus answers prayer;
There humbly fall before His feet,
For none can perish there.

Thy promise is my only plea,
With this I venture nigh;
Thou callest burdened souls to Thee,
And such, O Lord, am I.

Bowed down beneath a load of sin,
By Satan sorely pressed,
By war without and fears within,
I come to Thee for rest.

Be Thou my Shield and hiding Place,
That, sheltered by Thy side,
I may my fierce accuser face,
And tell him Thou hast died!

O wondrous love! to bleed and die,
To bear the cross and shame,
That guilty sinners, such as I,
Might plead Thy gracious Name.

"Poor tempest tossed soul, be still;
My promised grace receive";
'Tis Jesus speaks—I must, I will,
I can, I do believe.

—JOHN NEWTON
From *Olney Hymns*

The Veil in the Temple

This loose-hanging four-inch thick sixty feet by thirty feet curtain was there to keep sinful men out of the Most Holy Place. That thick imposing veil in the Holy of Holies symbolized that which separated sinful man from the holy presence of Yahweh. The *only* way sinful man could ever approach a most holy God is by means of blood. The veil shut out and kept everyone from further approach. The curtain hung there as if to say, "Thus far and no more."

The only individual who had permission from God to enter into the Most Holy Place was the high priest, and he could enter in behind the veil only on the Day of Atonement with blood of sacrifices to sprinkle on the veil and the Mercy Seat. No one could approach the LORD God without passing the brazen altar with the bloody sacrifice. That huge veil kept everyone out of the Most Holy Place. There it hung in the Temple on the day Christ died.

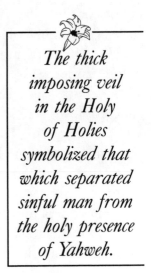

The thick imposing veil in the Holy of Holies symbolized that which separated sinful man from the holy presence of Yahweh.

Let's journey now to the afternoon of the crucifixion of Jesus. He has been hanging on the cross since around 9 A.M. Suddenly around noon a terrible thick darkness hung over Calvary and lasted for three hours. As this three hours was coming to an end at 3 P.M. Jesus cried out in God-forsakenness, "My God, My God, why have you forsaken Me?" It was the bitter cry of the divine sufferer experiencing the dregs of spiritual suffering as the Lamb of God. Jesus was voluntarily laying down His life for the redemption of the human race. It is beyond our human ability to understand the depths of His spiritual suffering in those three hours. He was God forsaken of God in the temporarily broken fellowship with His heavenly Father. Jesus' suffering was so terrible that God hid it from the eyes of depraved mankind.

Here is the awful climax of the suffering of the Son of God. He was "wounded for our transgressions" this Lamb of God. Christ was offering Himself as the "ransom for many." The precious blood of Jesus Christ redeemed us. In this spiritual suffering and death Jesus paid our sin debt to the righteousness of a holy God. Jesus on the cross "felt the way a lost sinner feels, without Himself having sinned," notes John Shepard.

> *The job Jesus came to do in His incarnation was completed in full.*

Some of the people thought Jesus was crying out for Elijah to come to His rescue. A Roman soldier hearing His cry, "I thirst," was moved by sympathy and took a sponge filled with sour vinegar wine and pressed it to the lips of Jesus. With His senses revived momentarily and His parched lips and throat moistened He gained strength to shout, "It is finished!" In that moment the work of redemption was completed. Nothing was left undone. It was a shout of triumph and victory. With a loud voice of a Conqueror He shouted, "Done!" "Complete!" "Finished!" The job He came to do in His incarnation was completed in full. The work of redemption was perfected and nothing else needed to be done by anyone. Jesus said, "Father, into Thy hands I commend My spirit" and He died. Jesus sent His spirit back to the Father. His death was a free act of will, handing His spirit back to God. "Jesus died a victor with a shout of triumph on His lips," says William Barclay.

In that horrible moment Matthew, Mark and Luke tell us the veil or curtain that separated the Holy Place from the Most Holy Place in the Temple was torn in two from the top to the bottom. "And behold, the veil of the temple was torn in two from top to bottom; and the earth shook and the rocks were split" (Matthew 27:51).

The veil or curtain referred to is the loose-hanging four-inch thick curtain that hung between the Holy Place and the Holy of Holies. There was something about the tear itself as the veil hung there in two parts that was obvious to anyone observing it that it was torn from the top. No man could have done it. Two men could not have torn it by grabbing hold of it at the center standing on the floor and pulling at it. The veil did not shake to pieces. The Temple was not damaged in any way that day. The timing of the split veil is the critical factor. The moment Jesus died the veil was torn from the top to the bottom and *then* the earth shook and rocks were split. No violence was done to the Temple or any of its quarters. It was not jerked apart by a couple of men.

The tearing of the veil was independent of the shaking of the earth. The ripping apart of the veil was the result of the shout from the cross by Jesus, "It is finished!" The same cry would be the cause of the earth to shake. At the moment Christ shouted the curtain was severed completely as if a great hand reached down and ripped it apart from the top to the bottom.

It was clearly cut by an invisible hand from top to bottom. No hand of sinful man tore the veil. Nothing was displaced in the Temple. Only the torn curtain was affected. There it hung in two pieces; split down through the middle. It was not randomly torn here and there. The veil was of such tough fabric and so woven that it could not have been rent in twain by an earthquake or falling of a lintel.

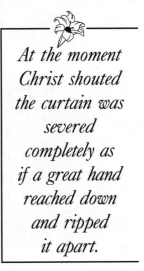

At the moment Christ shouted the curtain was severed completely as if a great hand reached down and ripped it apart.

Mark writes, "And Jesus uttered a loud cry, and breathed His last. And the veil of the temple was torn in two from top to bottom" (Mark 15:37–38). It is as if God in person acts, as any devoted Jewish father would have done standing by His own Son's deathbed. He rent His garments. The customary Jewish mourning gesture of a father was to tear his outer garment. Because God reached down and tore the veil in two we now have full and free entrance into the presence of God through His Son, Jesus Christ.

When the veil was torn that which kept man from God's presence was completely removed. Your sins and my sins have been totally removed and we can now enter into fellowship with God. Sin was the thing that separated man from God and Jesus Christ has completely and forever removed it for all who call upon His name. The way into the presence of God is open to all men everywhere. The veil is removed forever. The torn curtain was symbolically representing the way into the presence of God by the death of Jesus.

The torn veil says to every believer in Jesus Christ there is no valid reason why we should hesitate for one moment any time, anywhere to draw near to our Father in perfect freedom of spirit. That is the whole point; He wants us to come to Him often.

It was no minor tear of the curtain. The veil was bisected and could no longer function to keep people out of the Holy of Holies. Jesus Christ is the open door into the presence of God the Father. And there is no other door.

—WIL POUNDS
From Abide in Christ website

He Was Heard

In the days of old
The Priest would come
With a lifeless sacrifice,
While the crowd in anxious silence
Would wait outside.
As he entered in the temple,
They only hoped he would be heard.
God would give them a tomorrow,
And the priest would stay alive.

Their only chance,
Their only hope,
Would he be heard?
The only way
They might be saved,
Would he be heard?

In the fullness of promised time,
The final priest did some

And he offered up a living sacrifice.
Now we His children wait for Him
With hope and joyful praise,
For we know that God has heard Him,
For we know that He was raised.

He offered
Tearful prayers
And He was heard.
He offered up
His life
And He was heard.

So let us fix our eyes upon
The priest whom God did hear.
For the joy that was before Him,
He overcame the fear.
For once and all He paid the cost,
Enduring all the shame,
Taking up the cruel cross,
Ignoring all the pain.

The crowd is waiting outside the temple in silence. The signal has already been given. The high priest has gone into the Holy of Holies and, for the only time in the year allowed, has spoken the sacred name of God. At that signal the Jews assembled outside in the courtyard fall to their faces in respect and fear, since the priest and presumably the temple will be destroyed if he has spoken "the name" with impure lips.

The crowd awaits the high priest's return to the front of the temple with the announcement that the sacrifice has been accepted and that full forgiveness has been granted. The sacrifice he offers is for his sins and for the sins of the people. If he returns, all is well. If he does not return, the crowd outside will know he has been struck down in the temple and they will remain guilty, unclean, hopeless. He is their only hope.

In the book of Hebrews, the writer presents Jesus as our High Priest. The high priest in the Old Testament offered up blood that was "not his own," a lifeless sacrifice, but Jesus offered His own blood. His sacrifice was better because it was a living sacrifice, which was offered "once for all," not every year. And unlike the high priest, who served only for a specific period of time, Jesus' is an eternal priesthood (in the order of Melchizedek).

> *The sacrifice the priest offers is for his sins and for the sins of the people.*

—MICHAEL CARD
From *Immanuel: Reflections on the Life of Christ*

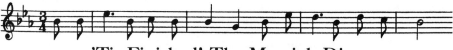

'Tis Finished! The Messiah Dies

'Tis finished! The Messiah dies,
Cut off for sins, but not His own:
Accomplished is the sacrifice,
The great redeeming work is done.

'Tis finished! all the debt is paid;
Justice divine is satisfied;
The grand and full atonement made;
God for a guilty world hath died.

The veil is rent in Christ alone;
The living way to heaven is seen;
The middle wall is broken down,
And all mankind may enter in.

The types and figures are fulfilled;
Exacted is the legal pain;

The precious promises are sealed;
The spotless Lamb of God is slain.

The reign of sin and death is o'er,
And all may live from sin set free;
Satan hath lost his mortal power;
'Tis swallowed up in victory.

Saved from the legal curse I am,
My Savior hangs on yonder tree:
See there the meek, expiring Lamb!
'Tis finished! He expires for me.

Accepted in the Well-beloved,
And clothed in righteousness divine,
I see the bar to heaven removed;
And all Thy merits, Lord, are mine.

Death, hell, and sin are now subdued;
All grace is now to sinners given;
And lo, I plead the atoning blood,
And in Thy right I claim Thy heaven!

—CHARLES WESLEY
From *Short Hymns*

The Torn Veil
(Excerpt)

All the Synoptic Gospels, in their accounts of Jesus' crucifixion, inform their readers that when Jesus had yielded up His spirit, the veil of the temple was torn in two. Matthew alone adds that the earth quaked and the rocks were split (27:51). The symbolical significance of this occurrence did not escape their attention, nor should it escape ours. We intend to show that the tearing of the temple veil has profound significance for the new covenant people of God.

The Significance of the Veil Itself

In order to understand and appreciate the significance of the torn veil, we first need to understand *the significance of the veil itself.* The veil they referred to was a thick veil made of woven linen that separated the holy place in the tabernacle from the most holy place. Into this most holy place, no one was allowed to enter except Israel's high priest. Even he could enter only once a year with the blood of a sacrifice. Only after he had made an offering for his sins could he offer the blood of a sacrifice for the sins the people had committed in ignorance. The plain significance of the linen curtain was that the old covenant could not reveal the way for the sinner's approach to God. After describing the physical arrangement of the tabernacle, the writer of the Epistle to the Hebrews discloses the symbolical significance that the Holy Spirit intended to convey by this arrangement. (Heb 9: 6–10).

> *Even the priest could enter the Holy of Holies only once a year with the blood of a sacrifice and only after he had made an offering for his own sins.*

No Access Under the Old Covenant

It does not require a wild imagination or inspired ingenuity to find a symbolical significance for the tabernacle veil. The text makes the Holy Spirit's intention concerning this matter very clear. It stood as a symbol of the old covenant's inability to reveal the way into God's holy presence.

The writer understood that Jehovah intended the old covenant to emphasize His absolute holiness and unbending righteousness (2:2; 10:27–31; 12:18–21, 29). While the first tabernacle stood and the old covenant remained in force, the way into God's holy presence remained hidden; . . . the way into the Most Holy Place had not yet been disclosed as long as the first tabernacle was still standing (Heb 9:8).

The Significance of the Torn Veil

The tearing of the temple veil is full of significance for the new covenant people of God. The radical shaking that accompanied this event (cf. Heb 12:25–29), as well as the event itself, bears eloquent testimony that the redemptive work of Christ effected far more than a mere change of administration within an overarching covenant of grace. His redemptive word was a divine intervention in history that inaugurated a new age; a new creation. Those who belong to this new creation are heirs of better promises that are granted by a new and better covenant. The old order has passed away, and the new order has come to stay.

A Notice of Unemployment

The tearing of the temple veil amounted to an unemployment notice. It was a public announcement to the priest of the Levitical order that their services were no longer needed. It said to them, You don't work here anymore! Another priest has risen who by His one act of sacrifice has accomplished what all you priests of the old order have failed to do. All your priestly service and all the sacrifices you have offered, continually, have failed to clear the sinner's conscience and give him bold access into God's presence. Those priests stand daily ministering and offering time after time the same sacrifices which can never take away sins; but He, having offered one sacrifice for sins for all time, SAT DOWN AT THE RIGHT HAND OF GOD, . . . (Heb 10:11–12). For the Law, since it has only a shadow of the good things to come and not the very form of things, can never by the same sacrifices year by year, which they offer continually, make perfect those who draw near (Heb 10:1). Isaac Watts wrote,

> *The tearing of the temple veil was an announcement to the priests of the Levitical order that their services were no longer needed.*

> *Not all the blood of beasts*
> *On Jewish altars slain,*
> *Could give the guilty conscience peace,*
> *Or wash away the stain:*

But Christ, the heav'nly Lamb
Takes all our sins away,
A sacrifice of nobler name
And richer blood than they.

Free Access Into God's Holy Presence

Everything about the law said stay away. Everything about the gospel says . . . **let us draw near** with a sincere heart in full assurance of faith, having our hearts sprinkled clean from an evil conscience and our bodies washed with pure water (Heb 10:22). Jesus, our great priest, has removed every obstacle that hindered our confident approach to God. Let us therefore approach God's gracious throne with confidence, that we may receive mercy and find grace that provides timely help for our needs (Heb 4:16).

Turn then my soul into thy rest;
The merits of thy great High Priest
Speak peace and liberty;
Trust in his efficacious blood,
Nor fear thy banishment from God,
Since Jesus died for thee.
———A. M. TOPLADY

———RANDAL SEVIER

Remember Me

Praying in the garden of Gethsemane,
Petitions penned with blood, sweat, and tears.
Crying, "Father, I have been obedient to You
For all of my 33 years."
"If it's possible, please take this cup from me,"
Said the suffering son.
"But if this be the only way, Dear Father,
Not my will, but Yours be done."

As He finished His urgent request to His Father
The soldiers burst onto the scene,
Seizing our Lord who was marked by a kiss—
Betrayed by a friend with a scheme.

They mocked Him, and beat Him,
And whipped Him for sport,
Sneering, "Hail, King of the Jews!"
They forced Him to walk while He carried His cross—
Could you have walked in His shoes?

Nails fashioned by hate were thrust through the hands
That had reached out in love to the world.
And our life that was lost once again was restored
As out of Christ's body blood spilled.

In the final dark hours as He hung there alone,
Divinely completing His task,
One question remained on His face wracked with pain,
"Why have you forsaken me?" He asked.

Then came His last words—"It is finished", He said,
As He breathed His last breath for you.
And the sky became dark, and the earth shook with fear
As the veil was torn in two.

He was wrapped in white linen and laid in a tomb
Possessed by a man of some fame
And a stone was placed in the door to that tomb
So secure, none would see Him again.

But our Heavenly Father is far greater still
Than any plan man could devise.
They discovered the stone was removed from that grave
For Hallelujah! Our Lord did arise!

So what's your response to this wondrous God
Who poured out His love on a cross?
If you were worth dying for, then He is worth living for.
Share God's love with a world that is lost.

—NAOMI MAIUZZO
From Sincerely Yours Christian
Poetry website

The Lion, the Witch, and the Wardrobe
(Excerpt)

It was quite definitely lighter now. Each of the girls noticed for the first time the white face of the other. They could see the mice nibbling away; dozens and dozens, even hundreds, of little field mice. And at last, one by one, the ropes were all gnawed through

The sky in the East was whitish by now and the stars were getting fainter—all except one very big one low down on the Eastern horizon. They felt colder than they had been all night. The mice crept away again.

The girls cleared away the remains on the gnawed ropes. Aslan looked more like himself without them. Every moment his dead face looked nobler, as the light grew and could see it better.

In the wood behind them a bird gave a chuckling sound. It had been so still for hours and hours that it startled them. Then another bird answered it. Soon there were birds singing all over the place.

It was quite definitely early morning now, not late night.

"I'm so cold," said Lucy.

So am I," said Susan. "Let's walk about a bit."

They walked to the Eastern edge of the hill and looked down. The one big star had almost disappeared. The country all looked dark grey, but beyond, at the very end of the world, the sea showed pale. The sky began to turn red. They walked to and fro more times than they could count between the dead Aslan and the Eastern ridge, trying to keep warm; and oh, how tired their legs felt. Then at last, as they stood for a moment looking out towards the sea and Cair Paravel (which they could now just make out) the red turned to gold along the line where the sea and the sky met and very slowly up came the edge of the sun. At that moment they heard from behind them a loud noise—a great cracking, deafening noise as if a giant had broken a giant's plate.

"What's that?" said Lucy, clutching Susan's arm.

"I—I feel afraid to turn round," said Susan; "something awful is happening."

"They're doing something worse to him," said Lucy. "Come on!" And she turned, pulling Susan with her.

The rising of the sun had made everything look so different—all the colours and shadows were changed—that for a moment they didn't see the important thing. Then they did. The Stone Table was broken into two pieces by a great crack that ran down it from end to end . . .

—C. S. Lewis

My Utmost for His Highest
(Excerpt)

"The cross was a superb triumph in which the foundations of hell were shaken. There is nothing more certain in time or eternity than what Jesus Christ did on the cross: He switched the whole of the human race back into a right relationship with God. He made Redemption the basis of human life, that is, He made a way for every son of man to get into communion with God."

—Oswald Chambers

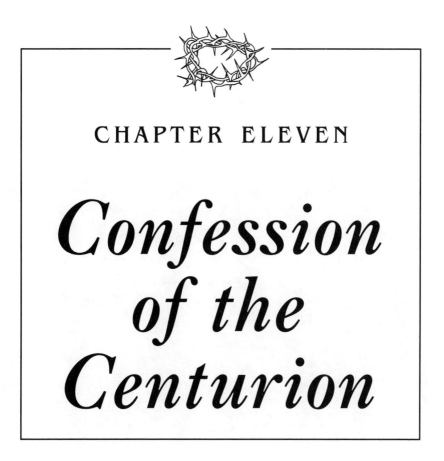

CHAPTER ELEVEN

Confession of the Centurion

Confession of the Centurion

MATTHEW 27:54

⁵⁴So when the centurion and those with him, who were guarding Jesus, saw the earthquake and the things that had happened, they feared greatly, saying, "Truly this was the Son of God!"

No Wonder They Call Him the Savior
(Excerpt)

"If it is true that a picture paints a thousand words, then there was a Roman centurion who got a dictionary full. All he did was see Jesus suffer. He never heard him preach or saw him heal or followed him through the crowds. He never witnessed him still the wind; he only witnessed the way he died. But that was all it took to cause this weather-worn soldier to take a giant step in faith.

That says a lot, doesn't it? It says the rubber of faith meets the road of reality under hardship. It says the trueness of one's belief is revealed in pain. Genuineness and character are unveiled in misfortune. Faith is at its best, not in three-piece suits on Sunday mornings or at V.B.S. on summer days, but at hospital bedsides, cancer wards and cemeteries.

Maybe that's what moved this old, crusty soldier. Serenity in suffering is a stirring testimony. Anybody can preach a sermon on a mount surrounded by daisies. But only one with a gut full of faith can live a sermon on a mountain of pain."

—MAX LUCADO

MAX LUCADO (1955–   )—Using his signature storytelling style, Max Lucado has sold over 15 million books. Currently, he is the pastor of Oak Hills Church of Christ in San Antonio, TX. He holds degrees from Abilene Christian University in Abilene, TX, including a Master of Biblical Studies. His engaging and captivating writings include three books that have won the Gold Medallion Christian Book of the Year Award. Lucado is one of the best-loved Christian authors of our day.

Christ's Desire for His Saints
(An Excerpt from a Communion Sermon
Preached on January 19, 1840)

"The wounds of Christ were the greatest outlets of his glory that ever were. The divine glory shone more out of his wounds than out of all his life before."

—ROBERT MURRAY MCCHEYNE

Six Hours One Friday
(Excerpt)

"Perhaps it was a similar look that stirred the soul of the soldier during those six hours one Friday.

He was uneasy. He had been since noon.

It wasn't the deaths that troubled him. The centurion was no stranger to finality. Over the years he'd grown calloused to the screams of the crucified. He'd mastered the art of numbing his heart. But this crucifixion plagued him.

The day began as had a hundred others—dreadfully. It was bad enough to be in Judea, but it was hell to spend hot afternoons on a rocky hill supervising the death of pickpockets and rabble-rousers. Half the crowd taunted, half cried. The soldiers griped. The priests bossed. It was a thankless job in a strange land. He was ready for the day to be over before it began.

He was curious at the attention given to the flatfooted peasant. He smiled as he read the sign that would go on the cross. The condemned looked like anything but a king. His face was lumpy and bruised. His back arched slightly and his eyes faced downward. "Some harmless hick," mused the centurion. "What could he have done?"

Then Jesus raised his head. He wasn't angry. He wasn't uneasy. His eyes were strangely calm as they stared from behind the bloody mask. He looked at those who knew him—moving deliberately from face to face as if he had a word for each.

For just a moment he looked at the centurion—for a second, the Roman looked into the purest eyes he'd ever seen. He didn't know what the look meant. But the look made him swallow and his stomach feel empty. As he watched the soldier grab the Nazarene and yank him to the ground, something told him this was not going to be a normal day.

As the hours wore on, the centurion found himself looking more and more at the one on the center cross. He didn't know what to do with the Nazarene's silence. He didn't know what to do with his kindness.

But most of all, he was perplexed by the darkness. He didn't know what to do with the black sky in mid-afternoon. No one could explain it . . . no one even tried. One minute the sun—the next the darkness. One minute the heat, the next a chilly breeze. Even the priests were silenced.

Jesus' eyes were strangely calm as they stared from behind the bloody mask that was his face.

For a long while the centurion sat on a rock and stared at the three silhouetted figures. Their heads were limp, occasionally rolling from side to side . . . . The jeering was silent . . . eerily silent. Those who had wept, now waited.

Suddenly the center head ceased to bob. It yanked itself erect. Its eye opened in a flash of white. A roar sliced the silence. "It is finished." It wasn't a yell. It wasn't a scream. It was a roar . . . a lion's roar. From what world that roar came the centurion didn't know, but he knew it wasn't this one.

The centurion stood up from the rock and took a few paces toward the Nazarene. As he got closer he could tell that Jesus was staring into the sky. There was something in his eyes that the soldier had to see. But after only a few steps, he fell. He stood and fell again. The ground was shaking, gently at first and now violently. He tried once more to walk and was able to take a few steps and then fall . . . at the foot of the cross.

> *"This was no carpenter," the centurion spoke under his breath. "This was no peasant. This was no normal man."*

He looked up into the face of this one near death. The King looked down at the crusty old centurion. Jesus' hands were fastened—they couldn't reach out. His feet were nailed to timber, they couldn't walk toward him. His head was heavy with pain, he could scarcely move it. But his eyes . . . they were afire.

They were unquenchable. They were the eyes of God.

Perhaps that is what made the centurion say what he said. He saw the eyes of God. He saw the same eyes that had been seen by a near-naked adulteress in Jerusalem, a friendless divorcee in Samaria, and a four-day-dead Lazarus in a cemetery. The same eyes that didn't close upon seeing man's futility, didn't turn away at man's failure, and didn't wince upon witnessing man's death.

"It's all right," God's eyes said. "I've seen the storms and it's still all right."

The centurion's convictions began to flow together like rivers. "This was no carpenter," he spoke under his breath. "This was no peasant. This was no normal man."

He stood and looked around at the rocks that had fallen and the sky that had blackened. He turned and stared at the soldiers as they stared at Jesus with frozen faces. He turned and watched as the eyes of Jesus lifted and looked toward home. He listened as the parched lips parted and the swollen tongue spoke for the last time.

"Father, into your hands I entrust my spirit."

Had the centurion not said it, the soldiers would have. Had the centurion not said it, the rocks would have—as would have the angels, the stars, even the demons. But he did say it. It fell to a nameless foreigner to state what they all knew.

"Surely this man was the Son of God."

Six hours on one Friday. Six hours that jut up on the plain of human history like Mount Everest in a desert. Six hours that have been deciphered, dissected, and debated for two thousand years.

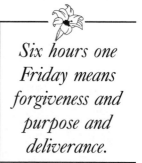

What do these six hours signify? They claim to be the door in time through which eternity entered man's darkest caverns. They mark the moments that the Navigator descended into the deepest waters to leave anchor points for his followers.

Six hours one Friday means forgiveness and purpose and deliverance.

What does that Friday mean?

For the life blackened with failure, that Friday means forgiveness.

For the heart scarred with futility, that Friday means purpose.

And for the soul looking into this side of the tunnel of death, that Friday means deliverance.

Six hours. One Friday.

What do you do with those six hours on that Friday?

—MAX LUCADO

Dr. Maclear's New Testament History
(Excerpt)

A centurion watched the crucifixion of our Lord (Matt. 27:54; Luke 23:47), and when he saw the wonders attending it, exclaimed, "Truly this man was the Son of God." The centurions mentioned in the New Testament are uniformly spoken of in terms of praise, whether in the Gospels or in the Acts. It is interesting to compare this with the statement of Polybius (vi. 24), that the centurions were chosen by merit, and so were men remarkable not so much for their daring courage as for their deliberation, constancy, and strength of mind.

Lord Jesus God and Man
(Inspired by "Surely this man was the Son of God.")

Lord Jesus, God and Man,
For love of man a Child,
The very God, yet born on earth
Of Mary undefiled.
Lord Jesus, God and Man,
In this our festal day
To Thee for precious gifts of grace
Thy ransomed people pray.
We pray for childlike hearts,
For gentle, holy love,
For strength to do Thy will below
As angels do above.
We pray for simple faith,
For hope that never fails,
For true communion evermore
With all Thy blessed saints.
On friends around us here
O let Thy blessing fall;
We pray for grace to love them well,
But Thee beyond them all.
O joy to live for Thee!
O joy in Thee to die!
O very joy of joys to see
Thy face eternally!
Lord Jesus, God and Man,
We praise Thee and adore,
Who art with God the Father One,
And Spirit evermore.

—HENRY W. BAKER

The Centurion: Voice of Affirmation

"Tough, disciplined, accustomed to hardship and rough living, he was a man marked more by violence and warfare than by humility and compassion. It would be extremely hard to put a dent in *his* emotional armor. Then he stood at the foot of a cross presiding over yet another execution, and he saw a man die in a way that no other had. It pierced this centurion's hardened heart and prompted him to recognize that Jesus was indeed who He claimed to be."

—WOODROW KROLL
From *The Twelve Voices of Easter*

Mighty in Spirit

He had never seen it this dark so early in the day. Something different was happening some momentous event. Whatever it was, he was sure it had nothing to do with him. He was just doing his job. A shiver of anticipation ran through him.

His occupation was to execute outlaws in Palestine. The breastplate that covered his heart bore the seal of his master Caesar, the Emperor of Rome. He gladly would have slashed the heart of anyone who stood against Caesar, for Caesar was like a god to him. There was honor in being a Centurion, a mighty warrior in charge of 100 brave soldiers trained to defend the Roman Empire. He knew how to wield a sword and shoot an arrow. He knew how to make his heart like a stone as He watched foreign soldiers die by his hand. It was his profession.

He looked at the crosses standing as monuments to an ever-raging war. Innumerable sentences had been carried out there for the purpose of protecting the peace. He stood vigil as death wrestled the spirits of men for days and reduced them to a mass of lifeless flesh. Many uttered their last words in languages unknown to him. Some pleaded for mercy. Some screamed angrily. Some could not speak at all. How he wrestled with the memory of them.

Today it seemed as if everyone was screaming. The prisoners, the temple officials. Even the Centurions own men were jeering at one of the criminals unmercifully. An immense crowd had turned out to witness the execution of a Man whose crime was written on the notice above His head. He was not a thief or murderer but King of the Jews.

> *Even though the Centurion stood for everything that put Christ on that splintered Roman cross, Jesus forgave him.*

The prisoner was Galilean, and He had made the mistake of angering the religious leaders. The accusations had no real basis, but who cared? Keep the peace of Caesars Empire. It was not his choice; those were his orders.

But this Galilean was like none the Centurion had ever seen. Stripped naked, whipped, bleeding, with a crown of thorns gouging His skull. The Galilean didn't fight as the others. Nor did He beg or curse. Soldiers tried to steal His dignity but couldn't. Even after they had cast lots for His cloak and had coated His dry tongue with vinegar, the Galilean wasn't condemning and He never pleaded for mercy.

In fact, this Galilean called Christ did something that tore at the Centurions stone-cold heart. He forgave. In all the Centurions years of watching people die on crosses, Jesus was the only One who ever offered mercy to him. Jesus forgave him. Even though he stood for everything that put Christ on that splintered Roman cross Jesus forgave him.

Now the Centurion watched as the Galilean labored painfully for breath. How he wanted to call out to accept the forgiveness! But to call out would mean challenging Caesar. To speak in favor of the King of the Jews would mark him a traitor. To ask this prisoner for life would mean his own death.

Then the Galilean cried out, "Father, into your hands I commit My spirit" (Luke 23:46). And it was over. He no longer labored. His Spirit's moment of release led to chaos as the earth began to quake and tombs burst open.

It was true. Everything the Centurion had heard about Jesus' preaching, healing, and miracles—it was all true. Regardless of Caesar, regardless of the Centurion's own fate, Jesus was the Messiah. In that moment he could utter only one confession, "Surely this was the Son of God." (Mark 15:39)

To be mighty in spirit is to recognize who Jesus is. The Centurion did. The Centurion viewed the criminals on crosses as you might look upon a convict on death row. Yet when he saw Jesus, he knew something was different. When he looked upon the Savior, neither his past nor his situation mattered. He simply couldn't deny the truth. The word of the warrior was that he had seen the Savior. He confessed that he had witnessed the Christ. Two thousand years later it is still possible to look upon Jesus, the resurrected Son of God.

What will be your confession?

—JENNY ROSANIA
Staff Writer for InTouch Ministries

INTOUCH MINISTRIES—Dr. Charles Stanley became the pastor of First Baptist Church in Atlanta, Georgia in 1971. Within the next three years, a television and syndicated radio program was aired nationwide. Today, the InTouch media reaches every nation on earth. More than 600,000 audios and 84,000 videos were produced last year, and more than 10 million *InTouch* magazines have been distributed around the world. The InTouch website at www.intouch.org strives to tell "the story of penetrating the human soul with the Word of God so that all who view or listen can grow to spiritual maturity and make a godly impact on the world . . ."

Sermon LXXIII. [CXXIII. Ben.]
(On Jesus as the Son of God)

". . . He then Who could do so great things, was hungry, and athirst, was wearied, slept, was apprehended, beaten, crucified, slain. This is the way; walk by humility, that thou mayest come to eternity. Christ-God is the Country whither we go. Christ-Man is the Way whereby we go. To Him we go, by Him we go; why fear lest we go astray? He departed not from the Father; and came to us. He sucked the breasts, and contained the world. He lay in a manger, and He fed the angels. God and man, the same God Who is Man, the same Man Who is God . . ."

—St. Augustine

Calvin's Commentaries
(Excerpt)

As Luke mentions the lamentation of the people, the centurion and his soldiers were not the only persons who acknowledged Christ to be the Son of God; but the Evangelists mention this circumstance respecting him for the purpose of heightening their description: for it is wonderful, that an irreligious man, who had not been instructed in the Law, and was ignorant of true religion, should form so correct a judgment from the signs which he beheld. This comparison tends powerfully to condemn the stupidity of the city; for it was an evidence of shocking madness, that when the fabric of the world shook and trembled, none of the Jews were affected by it except the despised rabble. And yet, amidst such gross blindness, God did not permit the testimonies which he gave respecting his Son to be buried in silence. Not only, therefore, did true religion open the eyes of devout worshippers of God to perceive that from heaven God was magnifying the glory of Christ, but natural understanding compelled foreigners, and even soldiers, to confess what they had not learned either from the law or from any instructor.

> *The centurion and his soldiers were not the only persons who acknowledged Christ to be the Son of God.*

When Mark says that the centurion spoke thus, because Christ, when he had uttered a loud voice, expired, some commentators think that he intends to point out the unwonted strength which remained unimpaired till death; and certainly, as the body of Christ was almost exhausted of blood, it could not happen, in the ordinary course of things, that the sides and the lungs should retain sufficient rigor for uttering so loud a cry. Yet I rather think that the centurion intended to applaud the unshaken perseverance of Christ in calling on the name of God. Nor was it merely the cry of Christ that led the centurion to think so highly of him, but this confession was extorted from him by perceiving that his extraordinary strength harmonized with heavenly miracles.

> *Perhaps the centurion intended to applaud the unshaken perseverance of Christ in calling on the name of God.*

The words, he feared God, must not be so explained as if he had fully repented. It was only a sudden and transitory impulse, as it frequently happens, that men who are thoughtless and devoted to the world are struck with the fear of God, when he makes an alarming display of his power; but as they have no living root, indifference quickly follows, and puts an end to that feeling. The centurion had not undergone such a change as to dedicate himself to God for the remainder of his life, but was only for a moment the herald of the divinity of Christ.

When Luke represents him as saying no more than certainly this was a righteous man, the meaning is the same as if he had plainly said that he was the Son of God, as it is expressed by the other two Evangelists. For it had been universally reported that Christ was put to death, because he declared himself to be the Son of God. Now when the centurion bestows on him the praise of righteousness, and pronounces him to be innocent, he likewise acknowledges him to be the Son of God; not that he understood distinctly how Christ was begotten by God the Father, but because he entertains no doubt that there is some divinity in him, and, convinced by proofs, holds it to be certain that Christ was not an ordinary man, but had been raised up by God.

As to the multitudes, by striving their breasts, they expressed the dread of punishment for a public crime, because they felt that public guilt had been contracted by an unjust and shocking murder. But as they went no farther, their lamentation was of no avail, unless, perhaps, in some persons it was the commencement or preparation of true repentance. And since nothing more is described to us than the lamentation which

God drew from them to the glory of his Son, let us learn by this example, that it is of little importance, or of no importance at all, if a man is struck with terror, when he sees before his eyes the power of God, until, after the astonishment has been abated, the fear of God remains calmly in his heart.

—JOHN CALVIN

Behold the Man
(Excerpt)

"Out of all history you'll find but one world conqueror who came with clean hands—and those hands the soldiers pierced with iron spikes when they nailed the Nazarene to the cross."

—IRVIN S. COBB

IRVIN S. COBB (1876–1944)—Irvin Shrewsbury Cobb began his literary career as a reporter for the *Paducah Daily News* when he was 16 years old. In 1898, he became a reporter for the *Louisville Evening Post*, but returned to Paducah in 1901 to become managing editor of the *Paducah Democrat*. Later, he worked for the *New York Evening Sun* and the *Saturday Evening Post*. At career's end, Cobb was credited with movie roles, short stories, and humorous editorials in magazines and newspapers.

The Centurion's Testimony at Jesus' Death
(Luke 23:47–48)

The Roman centurion in charge of the execution was a professional executor who had never seen anything like this before. He watched how

Jesus conducted Himself in the midst of all the hostility and hatred. In His last moments Jesus' loud cry of "restful resignation" made a profound never to be forgotten affect upon that soldier. It was a "voluntary surrender" of His life into the Father's hands. This was a cry of confidence.

The centurion testified, "Certainly this was a righteous [innocent] man, the Son of God" (Mark 15:39; Luke 23:47). He was greatly impressed by the darkness, the earthquake (Matt. 27:54), and certainly the manner in which Jesus suffered and died. Never had he heard a victim praying for his enemies. This hardened Roman soldier must have been shocked when Jesus shouted and then instantly died, for victims of crucifixion often lingered for days and did not have the strength to speak.

> *The centurion was greatly impressed by the darkness, the earthquake, and certainly the manner in which Jesus suffered and died.*

—WIL POUNDS
From *Father into Thy Hands*

The Centurion's Final Thought
(2nd Stanza)

"Who was the guilty?
Who brought this upon thee?
Alas, my treason, Jesus, hath undone thee.
'Twas I, Lord Jesus,
I it was denied thee:
I crucified thee."

—JOHANN HEERMANN
From *Ah, Holy Jesus, How Has Thou Offended*

The Murder of Jesus
(Excerpt)

Scripture records a number of supernatural phenomena that occurred while Jesus hung on the cross. Those events constituted God's own supernatural commentary on the cross. They are further proof of the extraordinary importance of what was occurring that day just outside Jerusalem.

The routes to the city that day were jammed with pilgrims coming and going as they prepared to celebrate Passover. Few if any of them realized the vital truth that God's true Paschal Lamb was dying that very day to provide forgiveness for all the sins of all the saints of all time. It was the very focal point of redemptive history, and yet as far as Jerusalem was concerned on that day, relatively few were taking notice. And few who witnessed the murder of Jesus had any idea at all what was really taking place.

> *Few who witnessed the murder of Jesus had any idea at all what was really taking place.*

But then suddenly all nature seemed to stop and pay attention.

Perhaps the most important miracle that occurred at the moment of Jesus' death was the conversion of the centurion charged with overseeing the crucifixion. As Christ's atoning work was brought to completion, its dramatic saving power was already at work in the lives of those who were physically closest to Him. Matthew 27:54 says, "So when the centurion and those with him, who were guarding Jesus, saw the earthquake and the things that had happened, they feared greatly, saying, 'Truly this was the Son of God!' "

A Roman centurion was the commander of a hundred-man division (or a "century")—the basic building block of a Roman legion. There were about twenty-five legions in the entire Roman army worldwide. Each legion comprised six thousand men, divided into ten cohorts of six hundred men each. Each cohort had three maniples, and each maniple was divided into two centuries. Each century was commanded by a centurion. The centurions were usually career officers, hardened men of war.

Because this particular officer was with those guarding Jesus, it appears he is the very one who had been given charge of overseeing and carrying out the crucifixion of Christ—and probably the crucifixions of the two thieves as well. He and his men were close eyewitnesses to everything that had happened since Jesus was taken to the Praetorium. They had personally kept Him under guard from that point on. (It is even possible that the centurion and some of the men with him were also the same soldiers who arrested Jesus the night before. If so, they had been eyewitnesses from the very beginning of the entire ordeal.) They had seen how Jesus held His silence while His enemies hurled accusations at Him. These same soldiers had strapped him to a post for the scourging, and watched while He suffered even that horrific beating with quiet grace and majesty. They themselves had mercilessly taunted Him, dress-

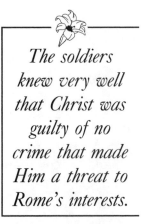

The soldiers knew very well that Christ was guilty of no crime that made Him a threat to Rome's interests.

ing Him in a faded soldier's tunic, pretending it was a royal robe. They had battered His head with a reed they gave Him as a mock scepter. These very same soldiers had also woven a crown of cruel thorns and mashed it into the skin of His scalp. They had spat on Him and taunted Him and mistreated Him in every conceivable fashion—and they had seen Him endure all those tortures without cursing or threatening any of His tormentors.

In all likelihood, the soldiers heard with their own ears when Pilate repeatedly declared Jesus' innocence. They knew very well that He was guilty of no crime that made Him a threat to Rome's interests. They must have been utterly amazed from the very beginning about how different He was from the typical criminal who was crucified. At first, they probably were inclined to write Him off as a madman. But by now they could see that He was not insane. He fit no category they had ever seen in the hundreds of crucifixions they had probably superintended.

Until now, the uniqueness of Christ had made no apparent impact whatsoever on these soldiers. They were hardened men, and Jesus' passivity made no difference in the way they treated Him. His obvious innocence had not gained any sympathy from them. They had showed Him no mercy.

> *When the soldiers saw the earthquake and the things that had happened, they feared greatly.*

They were professional soldiers, trained to follow orders. And so they had dutifully nailed Jesus' hands and feet to the cross. They had set the cross upright and dropped it into the hole dug for it. They had cast lots for Jesus' garments. And then they had sat down to watch Him die.

But Christ's death was unlike any crucifixion they had ever witnessed. They heard Him pray for His killers. They saw the noble way He suffered. They heard when He cried out to His Father. They experienced three full hours of supernatural darkness. And when that darkness was followed by an earthquake at the very moment of Christ's death, the soldiers could no longer ignore the fact that Christ was indeed the Son of God.

Mark suggests that there was something about the way Jesus cried out that struck the centurion as supernatural—perhaps the powerful volume of His cry, coming from someone in such a weakened condition. Mark writes, "When the centurion, who stood opposite Him, saw that He cried out like this and breathed His last, he said, 'Truly this Man was the Son of God!'" (Mark 15:39)

Matthew indicates that it was also the earthquake, coming at the exact moment of Jesus' final outcry, that finally convinced the centurion and his soldiers that Jesus was the Son of God: "When [they] saw the earthquake and the things that had happened, they feared greatly." (Matthew 27:54)

Notice that Matthew indicates all the soldiers had the same reaction. When the earthquake occurred they "feared greatly"—using a Greek word combination that speaks of extreme alarm. It's exactly the same expression Matthew used to recount how the three disciples reacted on the Mount of Transfiguration when Christ's glory was unveiled (17:6). This kind of fear was a typical reaction of people who suddenly realized the truth about who Jesus is. (cf. Mark 4:41, 5:33)

When the soldiers around the cross heard Jesus' exclamation, saw Him die, and then immediately felt the earthquake, it suddenly became all too clear to them that they had crucified the Son of God. They were stricken with terror. It wasn't merely the earthquake that they were afraid of. Rather they were terrified by the sudden realization that Jesus was innocent—and not merely innocent, but He was also precisely who He claimed to be. They had killed the Son of God. The centurion remembered the indictment of the Sanhedrin ("He made Himself the Son of God"—John 19:7), and having witnessed Jesus' death up close from beginning to end, he rendered his own verdict on the matter: "Truly this was the Son of God!"

> *The centurion and his soldiers with him were evidently the very first converts to Christ after His crucifixion.*

The word were evidently a true expression of faith. Luke says, "He glorified God, saying, 'Certainly this was a righteous Man!'" (Luke 23:47). So the centurion and his soldiers with him were evidently the very first converts to Christ after His crucifixion, coming to faith at precisely the moment He expired.

—JOHN MACARTHUR

The Jesus I Never Knew
(Excerpt)

When Jesus died, even a gruff Roman soldier was moved to exclaim, "Surely this man was the Son of God!" He saw the contrast all too clearly between his brutish colleagues and their victim, who forgave them in his dying gasp. The pale figure nailed to a crossbeam revealed the ruling powers of the world as false gods who broke their own lofty promises of piety and justice. Religion, not irreligion, accused Jesus; the law, not lawlessness, had him executed. By their rigged trials, their scourgings, their violent opposition to Jesus, the political and religious authorities of that day exposed themselves for what they were; upholders of the status quo, defenders of their own power only. Each assault on Jesus laid bare their illegitimacy.

—PHILIP YANCEY

The Drama of the Cross
(Excerpt)

Leaving Barabbas we moved around to the side of the cross. There we find the Roman Centurion. Acting on authority from Pontius Pilate,

> *The centurion knew this was no ordinary death.*

he is the commanding officer in this awful act. He is a big, strong man, hardened by many official acts of execution. No ordinary death would have made much of an impression upon him. But this was no ordinary death.

Perhaps this soldier was one of those commissioned to guard Jesus during the trials. He had seen the heartless scourging and heard the terrible mockery of Christ during the trials and even as He hung on the tree. This man knew that the greater part of the cursing crowd had never seen Jesus until now, in His hour of calamity. Yet they loaded Him with their curses and gave their sympathy to the thieves.

The other two who were crucified also turned on Him: "If thou be the Son of God, save thyself and us."

To the astonishment of the Centurion, the people laughed and applauded this statement. While everyone was listening for the reply, the thief on Christ's right was heard to say to the other, "Dost thou not fear God? We receive the due reward of our deeds, but this man hath done nothing amiss."

The soldier was astonished. In the midst of the hush which followed the first thief spoke again, this time to the Nazarene: "Lord, remember me when thou comest into thy kingdom."

The Centurion was struck with wonder. "Perhaps then, He is a king," he thought. "Perhaps His kingdom is not of this world and He is even now going to His kingdom. Yes, that is it! His kingdom is in heaven. Truly, this was the Son of God!"

—J. EUGENE WHITE

No Wonder They Call Him the Savior
(Excerpt)

The dialogue that Friday morning was bitter.

From the onlookers, "Come down from the cross if you are the Son of God!"

From the religious leaders, "He saved others but he can't save himself."

From the soldiers, "If you are the king of the Jews, save yourself."

Bitter words. Acidic with sarcasm. Hateful. Irreverent. Wasn't it enough that he was being crucified? Wasn't it enough that he was being shamed as a criminal? Were the nails insufficient? Was the crown of thorns too soft? Had the flogging been too short?

For some, apparently so.

Peter, a writer not normally given to using many descriptive verbs, says that the passersby "hurled" insults at the crucified Christ. They

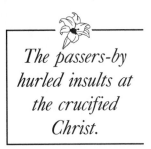

The passers-by hurled insults at the crucified Christ.

didn't just yell or speak or scream. They "hurled" verbal stones. They had every intention of hurting and bruising. "We've broken the body, now let's break the spirit!" So they strung their bows with self-righteousness and launched stinging arrows of pure poison.

Did you see what Jesus did not do? He did not retaliate. He did not bite back. He did not say, "I'll get you!" "Come on up here and say that to my face!" "Just wait until after the resurrection, buddy!" No, these statements were not found on Christ's lips.

Did you see what Jesus did do? He "entrusted himself to him who judges justly." Or said more simply, he left the judging to God. He did not take on the task of seeking revenge. He de-

Serenity in suffering is a stirring testimony.

manded no apology. He hired no bounty hunters and sent out no posse. He, to the astounding contrary, spoke on their defense. "Father, forgive them; for they do not know what they are doing."

Yes, the dialogue that Friday morning was bitter. The verbal stones were meant to sting. How Jesus, with a body wracked with pain, eyes blinded by his own blood, and lungs yearning for air, could speak on behalf of some heartless thugs is beyond my comprehension. Never, never have I seen such love. If ever a person deserved a shot at revenge, Jesus did. But he didn't take it. Instead he died for them.

There was something about the crucifixion that made every witness either step toward it or away from it. It simultaneously compelled and repelled.

And today, two thousand years later, the same is true. It's the watershed. It's the Continental Divide. It's Normandy. And you are either on one side or the other. A choice is demanded . . . On which side are you?

If it is true that a picture paints a thousand words, then there was a Roman centurion who got a dictionary full. All he did was see Jesus suffer. He never heard him preach or saw him heal or followed him through the crowds. He never witnessed him still the wind; he only witnessed the way he died. But that was all it took to cause this weather-worn soldier to take a giant step in faith. "Surely this was a righteous man."

Maybe that's what moved this old, crusty soldier. Serenity in suffering is a stirring testimony. Anybody can preach a sermon on a mount surrounded by daisies. But only one with a gut full of faith can *live* a sermon on a mountain of pain.

—MAX LUCADO

Quote

"Yes, if the life and death of Socrates were those of a sage, the life and death of JESUS are those of a God."

—JEAN JACQUES ROUSSEAU

An Example Without Rival
(. . . *Surely He Was the Son of God!*)

The character of Christ is singularly fitted to call forth the heart, to awaken love, admiration and moral delight. As an example it has no rival. As an evidence of his religion, perhaps it yields to no other proof; perhaps no other has so often conquered unbelief. The character of Christ is a strong confirmation of the truth of his religion.

The more we contemplate Christ's character, as exhibited in the Gospel, the more we shall be impressed with its genuineness and reality. It was plainly drawn from the life. The narratives of the Evangelists set before us the most extraordinary being who appeared on earth, and yet they are as artless as the stories of childhood. The Evangelists write with a calm trust in his character, with a feeling that it needed no aid from their hands, and with a deep veneration, as if comment or praise of their own were not worthy to mingle with the recital of such a life.

The character of Christ, taken as a whole, is one which could not have entered the thoughts of man, could not have been imagined or feigned it bears every mark of genuineness and truth it ought therefore to be acknowledged as real and of divine origin.

When I consider him, not only as possessed with the consciousness of an unexampled and unbounded majesty, but as recognizing a kindred nature in all human beings, and living and dying to raise them to a participation of his divine glories; and when I see him under these views allying himself to men by the tenderest ties, embracing them with a spirit of humanity, which no insult, injury, or pain could for a moment repel or overpower, I am filled with wonder as well as reverence and love. I felt that this character is not of human invention, that it was not assumed through fraud, or struck out by enthusiasm; for it is infinitely above their reach. When I add this character of Jesus to the other evidences of his religion, it gives to what before seemed so strong, a new and vast accession of strength. The character of Jesus is not fiction; he was what he claimed to be, and what his followers attested. Nor is this all. Jesus not only was, he is still the SON OF GOD, the Saviour of the world. He exists now; he has entered that Heaven to which he always looked forward on earth. There he lives and reigns.

—WILLIAM ELLERY CHANNING

> *The more we contemplate Christ's character, the more we shall be impressed with its genuineness and reality.*

According to Luke
(Excerpt)

Now the centurion in charge of the execution squad was merely doing his duty, and may at first have taken little interest in the issue at stake between Jewish leaders and Jesus, beyond being aware that it involved certain religious questions. The darkness obviously deepened his interest and set the crucifixion for him in a profound context. Luke does not tell us of Christ's cry of dereliction; he records simply the confidence and peace with which Christ went to meet God, as a son going to his Father (see 23:46). It was this that finally decided things for the centurion. "Surely this was a righteous man," he said; right not only in his dispute with the Jewish religious leaders, but right in relation with God. A man who could die like that in those circumstances and conditions must be right.

—DAVID GOODLING

On Jesus as the Son of God

To the senses, Jesus was the son of man: In Science, man is the son of God. The material senses could not recognize the Christ, or Son of God: it was Jesus' approximation to this state of being that made him the Christ-Jesus, the Godlike, the anointed.

—MARY BAKER EDDY

MARY BAKER EDDY (1821–1910)—Mary Baker Eddy was born in New England in 1821, and until 1862, she was practically an invalid from pain and ill health. She sought healing through every medical avenue available during that era, but it wasn't until she became a patient of Phineas Parkhurst Quimby, that she experienced some relief through his "medicine-free" approach to treating patients. Her improvement was dramatic, and she was drawn to the words Jesus spoke to the woman healed after a twelve-year illness—"Thy faith hath made thee whole." Another dramatic event occurred a few years later when she fell and struck her head on the ice. She was all but dead and fearing that her life on earth was about to end, she asked for a Bible. Suddenly, she felt the presence of God upon her and rose from the bed cured. From these experiences, Mrs. Eddy began to understand the "Science of Christianity," which she named Christian Science.

A Word with You
(Excerpt)

Now you'll have to climb a hill with me, it's called skull hill—that's outside the city of Jerusalem—and there you will find the one and only Son of God battered and bleeding on a Roman cross. We are going to take our place next to a Roman officer, in fact he's the man personally in charge of the execution of Jesus Christ. He's a tough, hardened executioner. He's about to speak, you need to hear what he is saying. *Mark 15:39—"And when the centurion, who stood there in front of Jesus, heard His cry and saw how He died, he said, 'Surely this was the Son of God!'"* The executioner! This is the Son of God! He didn't believe that when he came there that day, but he leaves there believing that. What changed his heart? Well, it says, *"he saw how He died."* He heard him say, "Father, forgive them." And he knew He was forgiving those who were responsible for His death. The centurion said, "Man that's me he's forgiving." Well, I know that it was me too.

—RON HUTCHCRAFT

When the Cross Returns

There is a storm coming up. I can hear its distant roar gathering strength as a wail that travels over wide fields. The waves roll on, uniform, equal in height and shape. With the waves pass the armies of slaves. There is struggle but no hope of victory. Chained together, they march to the end of the earth.

> *When the strong torture the weak, the head of the Man on the Cross sinks deeper on the tired breast.*

Now I feel the air growing colder. A Cross comes into sight. I hear the groans of the Man on the Cross. I see the blood on His face. He turns His head from side to side in nameless pain. His lips move. Hear! He speaks: "Eli, Eli, lama sabachtani!" A dark mist descends. The song of the birds is silenced, and the forests cease their rustling. The moon's rays are frozen, and the earth stands still. There is nothing but the wood and the Man who suffers on the Cross in eternal torment. The river moves on, but the Cross remains, now as a vague vision that recedes in the night, then moving forward in stark reality.

When the strong torture the weak, when the poor cry for bread, when the innocent languish in dungeons, when mothers go insane because they see their children die, when the outcasts roam in the wilderness, when the soldiers go to battle, when those who sit in darkness pray for light, the Cross returns, and the head of the Man on the Cross sinks deeper on the tired breast.

—PIERRE VAN PAASSEN
From *Behold the Man*

PIERRE VAN PAASSEN (1895–1968)—Pierre van Paassen was a Dutch-born American journalist and an active non-Jewish supporter of Jewish causes during the era of the Holocaust. In 1923, he began his lifelong attachment to Zionism. His most famous book, *Days of Our Years*, was published in 1939.

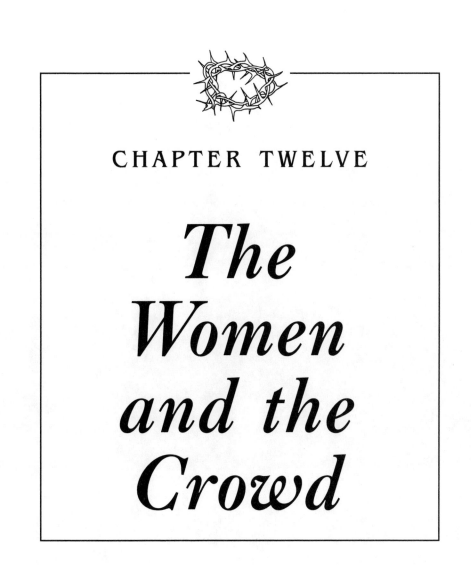

CHAPTER TWELVE

The Women and the Crowd

CHAPTER · TWELVE

The Women and the Crowd

MARK 15:40–41
⁴⁰*There were also women looking on from afar, among whom were Mary Magdalene, Mary the mother of James the Less and of Joses, and Salome,* ⁴¹*who also followed Him and ministered to Him when He was in Galilee, and many other women who came up with Him to Jerusalem.*

LUKE 23:48–49
⁴⁸*And the whole crowd who came together to that sight, seeing what had been done, beat their breasts and returned.*

Mary

Mary, when that little child
    Lay upon your heart at rest,
Did the thorns, Maid-mother mild,
    Pierce your breast?

Mary, when that little child
    Softly kissed your cheek benign,
Did you know, O Mary mild,
    Judas' sign?

Mary, when that little child
   Cooed and prattled at your knee,
Did you see with heartbeat wild,
   Calvary?

              —ROSE TRUMBULL
                From _Masterpieces of_
                Religious Verse

Stabat Mater
("The Mother Was Standing")

His mother stood there by the cross
Where her son was hanging,
His anguish sharing.
A sword pierced through her heart.

Though blessed and set apart
As mother of God's son,
Yet how great her painful sighing
To watch her child's slow dying.

Can there be one so cold
Who, seeing Christ's mother standing there,
Could watch her unconcernedly?
Not sorrowful himself, but hard and bold?

Not sharing her grief
To see him sliced by whips,
Split by nails,
In torment for our own sins and ills?
Her sweet son,
Abandoned, alone?

Mother, love's spring,
Pour out your pain on me
That with you I may mourn.
Make my heart burn
That I might love him too
And so bring joy to him and you.

O holy mother, drive the nails
Deep into my heart!
His wounds and dying—for whom else but me?
Let torment make us one,
Not drive us apart!

And may I also stand with you
Beside this cross,
Crying your tears,
Mourning your loss,
My life through.

Virgin above all virgins!
Do not shrug me away!
Wound me with his wounds.
Make me a drunkard of his cross
And of his blood—
My defense from fire and flame
On Judgment Day.

O Jesus, when it's my time to die,
Grant that through your mother's love
I might gain a place with you above.

Though my body fall away,
Lift my soul
To Paradise's eternal day!

—JACAPONE DA TODI
From *Divine Inspiration:*
The Life of Jesus in World Poetry

JACAPONE DA TODI (1228?–1306)—Todi was a Franciscan poet who was an extraordinary man, although little is known about his life. What is conjectured is that he was born into a noble family and might have studied law. There is one particular story that tells of his wife dying tragically at a festival. He was changed by the incident, abandoned his profession as an advocate and, wearing the habit of a Franciscan Tertiary, roamed the country for 10 years. His life was difficult, and at times, his behavior was bizarre, but he was canonized by the Church and his prose and poems exist today as a testament of his faith.

Mark 15:40, 41

VII. There were some of his friends, the good women especially, that attended him (v. 40, 41); *There were women looking on afar off:* the *men* durst not be seen at all, the mob was so very outrageous; *Currenti cede furori—Give way to the raging torrent,* they thought, was good counsel now. The women durst not come near, but stood at a distance, overwhelmed with grief. Some of these women are here named. *Mary Magdalene* was one; she had been his patient, and owed all her comfort to his power and goodness, which rescued her out of the possession of seven devils, in gratitude for which she thought she could never do enough for him. *Mary* also was there, *the mother of James the little, Jacobus parvus,* so the word is; probably, he was so called because he was, like Zaccheus, little of stature. This Mary was the wife of Cleophas or Alpheus, sister to the virgin Mary. These women had followed Christ *from Galilee,* though they were not required to attend the feast, as the males were; but it is probably that they came, in expectation that his temporal kingdom would now shortly be set up, and big with hopes of preferment for themselves, and their relations under him. It is plain that the mother

> *Those that follow Christ in expectation of great things in this world may live to see themselves sadly disappointed.*

of Zebedee's children was so (Mt. 20:21); and now to see *him* upon a cross, whom they thought to have seen upon a throne, could not but be a great disappointment to them. Note, those that follow Christ, in expectation of great things in this world by him, and by the profession of his religion, may probably live to see themselves sadly disappointed.

—MATTHEW HENRY
From *Commentary on the Whole Bible*

To the Lady Magdalen Herbert, of St. Mary Magdalen

HER of your name, whose fair inheritance
    Bethina was, and jointure Magdalo,
An active faith so highly did advance,
    That she once knew, more than the Church did
      know,
The Resurrection ; so much good there is
    Deliver'd of her, that some Fathers be
Loth to believe one woman could do this ;
    But think these Magdalens were two or three.
Increase their number, Lady, and their fame ;
    To their devotion add your innocence ;
Take so much of th' example as of the name,
    The latter half ; and in some recompense,
That they did harbour Christ Himself, a guest,
    Harbour these hymns, to His dear Name address'd.

—JOHN DONNE
From *Poems of John Donne, Vol. I.*

The Three Marys at Castle Howard, in 1812 and 1837

The lifeless son—the mother's agony,
O'erstrained till agony refused to feel—
That sinner too I then dry-eyed could see;
For I was hardened in my selfish weal,
And strength and joy had strung my soul with steel.
I knew not then what man may live to be,
A thing of life, that feels he lives in vain—
A taper, to be quenched in misery!
Forgive me, then, Caracci! if I seek
To look on this, thy tale of tears, again;
For now the swift is slow, the strong is weak.
Mother of Christ! how merciful is pain!
But if I longer view thy tear-stained cheek,
Heart-broken Magdalen! my heart will break.

—Ebenezer Elliot
From *A Sacrifice of Praise*

The Lion, the Witch, and the Wardrobe
(Excerpt)

As soon as the wood was silent again Susan and Lucy crept out into the open hill-top. The moon was getting low and thin clouds were passing across her, but still they could see the shape of the great Lion lying dead in his bonds. And down they both knelt in the wet grass and kissed his cold face and stroked his beautiful fur—what was left of it—and cried till they could cry no more. And then they looked at each other and held each other's hands for mere loneliness and cried again; and then again were silent. At last Lucy said,

"I can't bear the look of that horrible muzzle. I wonder could we take it off?"

So they tried. And after a lot of working at it (for their fingers were cold and it was not the darkest part of the night) they succeeded. And when they saw his face without it they burst out crying again and kissed and fondled it and wiped away the blood and the foam as well as they could. And it was all more lonely and hopeless and horrid than I know how to describe.

> *When there are no tears left, you will know that there comes in the end a sort of quietness.*

"I wonder could we untie him as well?" said Susan presently. But the enemies, out of pure spitefulness had drawn the cords so tight that the girls could make nothing of the knots.

I hope no one who reads this book has been quite as miserable as Susan and Lucy were that night; but if you have been—if you've been up all night and cried till you have no more tears left in you—you will know that there comes in the end a sort of quietness. You feel as if nothing was ever going to happen again. At any rate that was how it felt to these two. Hours and hours seemed to go by in this dead calm, and they hardly noticed that they were getting colder and colder . . .

—C. S. LEWIS

My Lord, My Master, at Thy Feet Adoring

My Lord, my Master, at Thy feet adoring,
I see Thee bowed beneath Thy load of woe;
For me, a sinner, is Thy life blood pouring;
For Thee, my Savior, scarce my tears will flow.
Thine own disciple to the Jews has sold Thee,
With friendship's kiss and loyal word he came;

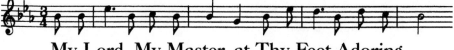

How oft of faithful love my lips have told Thee,
While Thou hast seen my falsehood and my shame.
With taunts and scoffs they mock what seems Thy weakness,
With blows and outrage adding pain to pain;
Thou art unmoved and steadfast in Thy meekness;
When I am wronged how quickly I complain!
My Lord, my Savior, when I see Thee wearing
Upon Thy bleeding brow the crown of thorn,
Shall I for pleasure live, or shrink from bearing
Whate'er my lot may be of pain or scorn?
O Victim of Thy love, O pangs most healing,
O saving death, O wounds that I adore,
O shame most glorious! Christ, before Thee kneeling,
I pray Thee keep me Thine for evermore.

—JACQUES BRIDAINE

The Celestial City from Christ's Triumph After Death
(Stanzas 30–43)

Here let my Lord hang upon his conquering lance,
And bloody armour with late slaughter warme,
And looking downe on his weake Militants,
Behold his Saints, 'midst of their hot alarme,
Hang all their golden hopes upon his arme.
And in this lower field dispacing wide,
Through windie thoughts, that would their sayles misguide,
Anchor their fleshly ships fast in his wounded side.

Here may the Band, that now in tryumph shines,
And that (before they were invested thus)
In earthly bodies carried heavenly mindes,
Pitcht round about in order glorious,

Their sunny Tents, and houses luminous,
All their eternall day in songs employing,
Joying their ends, without ende of their joying,
While their almightie Prince Destruction is destroying.

Full, yet without satietie, of that
Which whets and quiets greedy Appetite,
Where never Sunne did rise, nor ever sat,
But one eternall day, and endless light
Gives time to those, whose time is infinite,
Speaking with thought, obtaining without fee,
Beholding him, whom never eye could see,
And magnifying him, that cannot greater be.

How can such joy as this want words to speake?
And yet what words can speake such joy as this?
Far from the world, that might their quiet breake,
Here the glad Soules the face of beauty kisse,
Pour'd out in pleasure, on their beds of blisse.
And drunke with nectar torrents, ever hold
Their eyes on him, whose graces manifold,
The more they doe behold, the more they would behold.

Their sight drinkes lovely fires in at their eyes,
Their braine sweete incense with fine breath accloyes,
That on Gods sweating altar burning lies,
Their hungrie cares feede on their heav'nly noyse,
That Angels sing, to tell their untold joyes;
Their understanding naked Truth, their wills
The all, and selfe-sufficient Goodnesse fills,
That nothing here is wanting, but the want of ills.

No Sorrowe now hangs clouding on their browe,
No bloodless Maladie empales their face,
No Age drops on their hairs his silver snowe,
No Nakednesse their bodies doth embase,

No Povertie themselves, and theirs disgrace,
No feare of death the joy of life devours,
No unchast sleepe their precious time deflowrs,
No losse, no griefe, no change waite on their winged hours.

But now their naked bodies scorne the cold,
And from their eyes joy lookes, and laughs at paine,
The infant wonders how he came so old,
And old man how he came so young againe;
Still resting, though from sleepe they still refraine,
Where all are rich, and yet no gold they owe,
And all are Kings, and yet no Subjects knowe,
All full, and yet no time on foode they doe bestowe.

A heav'nly feast, no hunger can consume,
A light unseene, yet shines in every place,
A sound, no time can steale, a sweet perfume,
No windes can scatter, an intire embrace,
That no satietie can e'er unlace,
Ingrac'd into so high a favour, there
The saints, with their Beau-peers, whole worlds outwear,
And things unseene doe see, and things unheard doe hear.

Ye blessed soules, growne richer by your spoile,
Whose losse, though great, is cause of greater gaines,
Here may your weary Spirits rest from toyle,
Spending your endlesse ev'ning, that remaines,
Among those white flocks, and celestiall traines,
That feed upon their Sheapheards eyes, and frame
That heav'nly musique of so wondrous fame,
Psalming aloud the holy honours of his name.

Had I a voice of steel to tune my song,
Were every verse as smoothly fil'd as glasse,
And every member turned to a tongue,
And every tongue were made of sounding brasse,

Yet all that skill, and all this strength, alas,
Should it presume to gild, were misadvis'd,
The place, where David hath new songs devis'd,
As in his burning throne he sits emparadis'd.

—GILES FLETCHER THE YOUNGER
From *A Sacrifice of Praise*

The Encounter
(In Evil Long I Took Delight)

In evil long I took delight,
Unawed by shame or fear,
Till a new object struck my sight,
And stopped my wild career:
I saw One hanging on a tree
In agonies and blood,
Who fixed His languid eyes on me,
As near His cross I stood.

Sure never till my latest breath
Can I forget that look:
It seemed to charge me with His death,
Though not a word He spoke:
My conscience felt and owned the guilt,
And plunged me in despair;
I saw my sins His Blood had spilt
And helped to nail Him there.

Alas! I knew not what I did!
But now my tears are vain:
Where shall my trembling soul be hid?
For I the Lord have slain!
A second look He gave, which said,

'I freely all forgive;
This Blood is for thy ransom paid;
I die, that thou mayst live.'

Thus, while His death my sin displays
In all its blackest hue,
Such is the mystery of grace,
It seals my pardon too.
With pleasing grief, and mournful joy,
My spirit now is filled,
That I should such a life destroy,
Yet live by Him I killed!

—JOHN NEWTON
From *A Sacrifice of Praise*

The Annunciation and Passion

TAMELY, frail body, abstain to-day; to-day
My soul eats twice, Christ hither and away.
She sees Him man, so like God made in this,
That of them both a circle emblem is,
Whose first and last concur; this doubtful day
Of feast or fast, Christ came, and went away;
She sees Him nothing, twice at once, who's all;
She sees a cedar plant itself, and fall;
Her Maker put to making, and the head
Of life at once not yet alive, yet dead;
She sees at once the Virgin Mother stay
Reclused at home, public at Golgotha;
Sad and rejoiced she's seen at once, and seen
At almost fifty, and at scarce fifteen;
At once a son is promised her, and gone;

Gabriell gives Christ to her, He her to John;
Not fully a mother, she's in orbity;
At once receiver and the legacy.
All this, and all between, this day hath shown,
Th' abridgement of Christ's story, which makes one—
As in plain maps, the furthest west is east—
Of th' angels *Ave,* and *Consummatum est.*
How well the Church, God's Court of Faculties,
Deals, in sometimes, and seldom joining these.
As by the self-fix'd Pole we never do
Direct our course, but the next star thereto,
Which shows where th'other is, and which we say
—Because it strays not far—doth never stray,
So God by His Church, nearest to him, we know,
And stand firm, if we by her motion go.
His Spirit, as His fiery pillar, doth
Lead, and His Church, as cloud; to one end both.
This Church by letting those days join, hath shown
Death and conception in mankind is one;
Or 'twas in Him the same humility,
That He would be a man, and leave to be;
Or as creation He hath made, as God,
With the last judgment but one period,
His imitating spouse would join in one
Manhood's extremes; He shall come, He is gone;
Or as though one blood drop, which thence did fall,
Accepted, would have served, He yet shed all,
So though the least of His pains, deeds, or words,
Would busy a life, she all this day affords.
This treasure then, in gross, my soul, uplay,
And in my life retail it every day.

—JOHN DONNE
From *Poems of John Donne,*
Vol. I.

Easter Night

All night had shout of men and cry
Of woeful women filled His way;
Until that noon of sombre sky
On Friday, clamour and display
Smote Him; no solitude had He.
No silence, since Gethsemane.

Public was Death; but Power, but Might,
But Life again, but Victory,
Were hushed within the dead of night,
The shutter'd dark, the secrecy,
And all alone, alone, alone,
He rose again behind the stone.

—ALICE MEYNELL
From *A Sacrifice of Praise*

The Pilgrim's Progress
(Excerpt)

Gaius also proceeded, and said, "I will now speak on the behalf of women, to take away their reproach. For as death and the curse came into the world by a woman, so also did life and health: 'God sent forth his Son, made of a woman.' Yea, to show how much those that came after did abhor the act of their mother, this sex in the Old Testament coveted children, if haply this or that woman might be the mother of the Saviour of the world.

"I will say again, that when the Saviour was come, women rejoiced in him before either man or angel. I read not that ever any man did give unto Christ so much as one groat; but the women followed him, and ministered to him of their substance. It was a woman that washed his feet with tears, and a woman that anointed his body to the burial. They were women that wept when he was going to the cross, and women that followed him from the cross, and that sat by his sepulchre when he was buried. They were women that were the first with him at his resurrection-morn, and women that brought tidings first to his disciples that he was risen from the dead. Women, therefore, are highly favoured, and show by these things that they are sharers with us in the grace of life."

Women rejoiced in Jesus before either man or angel.

—JOHN BUNYAN

JOHN BUNYAN (1628–1688)—John Bunyan is one of the best-selling authors of all time. He was a religious leader whose influence has been felt throughout the world and who has given hope to thousands of people. A museum in his honor is located in Bedford, between Oxford and Cambridge. The church where Bunyan once preached, purchased in 1672, is presently known as Bunyan Meeting Free Church. Bunyan is the author of several books, including *Imprisonment, The Holy War,* and *The Life and Death of Mr. Badman.*

I Love to Tell the Story

I love to tell the story
Of unseen things above,
Of Jesus and his glory,
Of Jesus and his love.
I love to tell the story,
Because I know 'tis true;

It satisfies my longings
As nothing else can do.

I love to tell the story,
'Twill be my theme in glory
To tell the old, old story
Of Jesus and his love.

I love to tell the story;
More wonderful it seems
Than all the golden fancies
Of all our golden dreams.
I love to tell the story,
It did so much for me;
And that is just the reason
I tell it now to thee.

I love to tell the story;
'Tis pleasant to repeat
What seems, each time
I tell it, More wonderfully sweet.
I love to tell the story,
For some have never heard
The message of salvation
From God's own holy Word.

I love to tell the story;
For those who know it best
Seem hungering and thirsting
To hear it, like the rest.
And when in scenes of glory,
I sing the new, new song,

'Twill be the old, old story,
That I have loved so long.

—KATHERINE HANKEY
From *A Sacrifice of Praise*

Onlookers

"Sickness is a place . . . where there's no company,
where nobody can follow."
—FLANNERY O'CONNOR

Behind our shield of health, each
of us must sense another's anguish
second-hand; we are agnostic
in the face of dying. So Joseph
felt, observer of the push
and splash of birth, and even Mary,
mourner, under the cross's arm.

Only their son, and God's,
in bearing all our griefs
felt them first-hand, climbing
himself our rugged hill of pain.
His nerves, enfleshed, carried
the messages of nails, the tomb's
chill. His ever-open wounds
still blazon back to us the penalty
we never bore, and heaven
gleams for us more real,
crossed with that human blood.

—LUCI SHAW
From *A Sacrifice of Praise*

Crucifixion

In the crowd's multitudinous mind
   Terror and passion embrace,
Whilst the darkness heavily blind
   Hides face from horror-struck face;
And all men, huddled and dumb,
   Shrink from the death-strangled cry,
And the hidden terror to come,
   And the dead mean hurrying by.
White gleams from the limbs of the dead
   Raised high o'er the blood-stained sod,
And the soldier shuddered and said,
   'Lo, this was the Son of God.'
Nay, but all Life is one,
   A wind that wails through the vast,
And this deed is never done,
   This passion is never past.
When any son of man by man's blind doom
   Of any justest scaffold strangled dies,
Once more across the shadow-stricken gloom
   Against the sun the dark-winged Horror flies,
A lost voice cries from the far olive trees
   Weary and harsh with pain, a desolate cry,
What ye have done unto the least of these
   Is done to God in Heaven, for earth and sky,
And bird and beast, green leaves and golden sun,
   Men's dreams, the starry dust, the bread, the wine,
Rivers and seas, my soul and his, are one;
   Through all things flows one life austere, divine,—

Strangling the murderer you are slaying me,
  Scattering the stars and leaves like broken bread,
Casting dark shadows on the sun-lit sea,
  Striking the swallows and the sea-gulls dead,
Making the red rose wither to its fall,
  Darkening the sunshine, blasting the green sod,—
Wounding one soul, you wound the soul of all,
  The unity of Life, the soul of God.

—EVA GORE-BOOTH
From *A Sacrifice of Praise*

Near the Cross

Near the Cross her vigil keeping,
Stood the mother, worn with weeping,
Where He hung, the dying Lord:
Through her soul, in anguish groaning,
Bowed in sorrow, sighing, moaning,
Passed the sharp and piercing sword.

O the weight of her affliction!
Hers, who won God's benediction,
Hers, who bore God's Holy One:
O that speechless, ceaseless yearning!
O those dim eyes never turning
From her wondrous, suffering Son!

Who upon that mother gazing,
In her trouble so amazing,
Born of woman, would not weep?
Who of Christ's dear mother thinking,

While her Son that cup is drinking,
Would not share her sorrow deep?

For His people's sin chastised
She beheld her Son despised,
Bound and bleeding 'neath the rod;
Saw the Lord's Anointed taken,
Dying, desolate, forsaken,
Heard Him yield His soul to God.

Near Thy Cross, O Christ, abiding,
Grief and love my heart dividing,
I with her would take my place:
By Thy guardian Cross uphold me,
In Thy dying, Christ, enfold me
With the deathless arms of grace.

—UNKNOWN
From *Masterpieces of
Religious Verse*

Gethsemane

As Christ lay in Gethsemane,
Face down, with closed eyes,—
The breezes seemed nothing but sighs,
And a spring,
Reflecting the moon's pale face,
Murmuring its sorrow apace,—
That was the hour for the angel to bring,
In tears, from God, the bitter cup.

Then before Christ the cross rose up.
He saw his own body hanging there
Torn and wrenched, joints jutting where

The ropes stretched each limb back.
He saw the nails, the crown.
At each thorn a drop of blood hung down.
The thunder growled under its breath.
He heard a drip. Down the cross
Softly slid a whimper, then blurred out.
Christ sighed. In every pore
Sweat found a door.

The air went dark. In the grey ocean
A dead sun swam.
Through the murk he made out
The thorn-crowned head thrashing about.
Three forms lay at the cross's foot.
He saw them lying, grey as soot.
He heard the catching of their breath,
Saw how their trembling set their clothes in motion.
Was ever love as hot as his?
He knew them, knew them well.
His heart glowed.
Still harder his sweat flowed.

The sun's corpse vanished—just smoke, black day.
Cross and sighs both sank away.
A silence grimmer than a storm's roar
Swam through the starless paths of air.
No breath of life anywhere.
And, all around, a crater, burnt, empty,
And a hollow voice crying for pity,
"My God, my God, why have you forsaken me?"
Death's grip seized him.
He wept. His spirit broke.
Sweat turned blood. He shook.
His mouth formed words of pain and spoke.
"Father, if it's possible, let this hour
Pass me by."

A bolt of lightning cut the night!
In that light
Swam the cross, its martyr-symbols bright.
Hands by millions he saw reaching,
Hands large and small from near and far beseeching,
And hovering spark-like over the crown of thorn
The souls of millions yet unborn.
The murk slunk back into the ground,
While the dead in their graves their voices found.
In love's fulness Christ raised himself on high.
"Father," he cried, "not my
Will but yours be done."

The moon swam out in quiet blue.
Before him, on the dewy green,
A stem of lily stretched up its length.
Then out of the calyx-cup
An angel stepped
And gave him strength.

—ANNETTE VON DROSTE-HULSHOFF
From *Divine Inspiration: The Life of
Jesus in World Poetry*

ANNETTE VON DROSTE-HULSHOFF (1797–1848)—Annette von Droste-Hulshoff is the only woman writer whose works are included in anthologies and discussions of 19th century German literature. Consistently challenging traditional interpretations of her life and work, she never married, had very few friends, and was often ill. She didn't write for years at a time, and it wasn't until she was over 40 years of age that she began publishing her work—and that was only with the help of friends and after receiving approval from her mother. In 1837, she fell in love with a much younger man, who helped her secure her literary fame. Her best works were written during this time of love in her life. When he married another woman in 1843, she became ill and didn't write for her few remaining years.

Lament of Our Lady
Under the Cross

Hear me, my dears, this bleeding head
I want to lament before you turn;
listen to this affliction that
befell me on Good Friday.

Pity me, all of you, old and young,
The feast of blood will be my song.
I had a single son,
it is for him I weep.

A poor woman, I was rudely confused
when I saw my birthright in bitter blood.
Dreadful the moment and bloody the hour
when I saw the infidel Jew
beat and torment my beloved son.

Oh, son, sweet and singled-out,
share your pain with your mother.
I carried you near my heart, dear son.
I served you faithfully.
Speak to your mother. Console my great grief
now that you leave me and all my hopes.

Small boy, if you were only lower
I could give you a little help.
Your head hangs crooked: I would support it,
your dear blood flows; I would wipe it off.
And now you ask for a drink and a drink I
    would give you,
but I cannot reach your holy body.

Oh, angel Gabriel
where is that range of joy
you promised me would never change?
You said: "Virgin, you are filled with love,"
but now I am full of a great grief.
My body has rotted inside me and my bone moulder.

       —ANONYMOUS
         From *Divine Inspiration:*
         The Life of Jesus in World Poetry

Acknowledgments

W e have made every effort to locate the source for correct attribution to the publisher or writer. In the event that we did not provide the proper source, we welcome written documentation, and we will make corrections in future printings. If the material was not eligible for public domain, we selected quotations according to the generally accepted fair-use standards and practices. We greatly appreciate the publishers and authors who worked with us to create such a unique anthology about the death of Christ. The following acknowledgments are offered for these contributions.

Chapter One

Blackburn, Peter J. "Simon of Cyrene." *Between the Lines: Dialogues for Worship*. Testimonium Fellowship, 1992.

Chambers, Oswald. "What My Obedience to God Costs Other People." *My Utmost for His Highest*, 8.

Clephane, Elizabeth C. "Beneath the Cross of Jesus." *Family Treasury*, 1868.

Clow, W. M. Excerpt. *The Day of the Cross*. Baker Book House: Grand Rapids. 1955. 159–60.

Donne, John. "The Crosse." Public Domain.

Erdman, Charles R. Excerpt. *Remember Jesus Christ*. William B. Eerdmans: Grand Rapids, 1958. 92.

Gibran, Kahlil. "Simon the Cyrene." Public Domain.

Harris, Frank. "The King of the Jews." *The Passion Drama.* Creative Age Press, Inc.: New York. 1946. 331–333.

Ingraham, J. H. Excerpt. *The Prince of the House of David.* Hurst and Company Publishers, New York, 1950.

Kiefer, James E. Excerpt from *Simon of Cyrene—Cross Bearer.* Society of Archbishop Jesus website. http://justus.anglican.org/resources/bio/156.html

———. "Prayer." Society of Archbishop Jesus website. http://justus.anglican.org/resources/bio/156.html

Kresensky, Raymond. "Men Follow Simon." *Christ in the Poetry of Today.* The Womans Press: New York, 1917.

Linville, Larry R. "Simon of Cyrene." The Dramashare website. http://www.dramashare.org/scripts/simonof.htm

Ludwig, Emil. "For Simon of Cyrene." *Behold the Man.* Public Domain. 60.

Mackay, Rev. H. F. B. Excerpt. *Assistants at the Passion.* Morehouse Publishing Co.: Milwaukee. 131–139.

Munro, Edward and Mrs. M. Dearmer. "See Him in Raiment Rent." *The English Hymnal.* London: Oxford University Press, 1906.

Rimmer, D. D. Harry. Excerpt. *Voices from Calvary.* William B. Eerdmans: Grand Rapids, 1937.

Sangster, W. E. Excerpt. *They Met at Calvary.* Abingdon Press: New York/Nashville. 1956. 73.

Spurgeon, C. H. "April 5, Morning." *Morning and Evening.* Public Domain.

Stott, John. Excerpt. *The Cross of Christ.* Intervarsity Press: Downers Grove, 1986. 279.

Tittle, Ernest Fremont. Excerpt. *The Gospel According to Luke: Exposition & Application.* Harper & Brothers Publishers: New York. 1951. 256–257.

Venter, Frans. Excerpt. *Man from Cyrene.* Augsburg Fortress Publishers, 1962. 3–4, 221–223.

Wilson, Richard S. "St. Simon of Cyrene." The Franciscan Friars Third Order website. http://www.franciscanfriarstor.com/poetry/stf_stsimon.htm

Chapter Two

Alexander, Cecil F. "There Is a Green Hill Far Away." Public Domain.

Bernard of Clairvaux. "O Sacred Head, Now Wounded." Public Domain.

Bliss, Philip P. "Man of Sorrows! What a Name." Public Domain.

Card, Michael. Excerpt. *The Parable of Joy.* Thomas Nelson, Inc.: Nashville, 1995.

Crashaw, Richard. "Obsecration Before the Crucifix." *Complete Poetry.* Williams: New York, 1970.

Coleridge, Mary E. "The Cross." Public Domain.

Dolben, D. B. Untitled. Public Domain.

Hobbs, Herschel H. Excerpt. *Who Is This?* Broadman & Holman: Nashville, 1952.

Kelly, Thomas. "The Head That Once Was Crowned with Thorns." Public Domain.

Lewis, C. S. Excerpt. *The Lion, the Witch, and the Wardrobe.* Macmillan Publishing Company: New York, 1977.

Lucado, Max. Excerpt. *The Final Week of Jesus.* Multnomah Publishers, Inc.: Sisters, 1999.

Manning, Brennan. Excerpt. *Lion and Lamb.* Chosen Books, a division of Baker Book House: Grand Rapids, 1986.

Rosetti, Christina. *Untitled.* Public Domain.

Stott, John. Excerpt. *Basic Christianity.* Eerdmans Publishers Co.: Grand Rapids, 1977.

Via, Jr., Bernard S. "Pilate." *Seasons of Faith.* Brandylane Publishers, Inc.: Whitestone, VA.

————. "Timeless." *Seasons of Faith*. Brandylane Publishers, Inc.: Whitestone, VA.

————. "Good Friday." *Seasons of Faith*. Brandylane Publishers, Inc.: Whitestone, VA.

Watts, Isaac. "Christ Dying, Rising, and Reigning." *Lyric Poems, Book 1*. Public Domain.

Wesley, Charles. "And Can It Be?" *Stanzas 1, 2, 3, & 6*. Public Domain.

————. Untitled. *Great Joy by J. I. Packer*. Public Domain.

Yancey, Philip. Excerpt. *The Jesus I Never Knew*. Zondervan Publishing House: Grand Rapids, 2002.

Chapter Three

Casting of Lots. *The Thomas Nelson Open Bible Study Notes*. Thomas Nelson, Inc.: Nashville, 1975.

Farrar, Frederic William. "The Crucifixion." *The Life of Christ*. The World Publishing Company: Cleveland, 1913. 402–408.

Gire, Ken. Excerpt. *Moments with the Savior*. Zondervan Publishing House: Grand Rapids, 1998.

Goodspeed, Edgar, J. "The Crucifixion and the Resurrection." *A Life of Jesus*. Harper & Brothers, Publishers: New York, 1950. 217–219.

Hagg, Esther Lloyd. "His Garments." *Christ in Poetry*. Association Press: New York, 1952. 122.

Junus, Anna Maria. *Mary's Song*. The Family.com's One Great Family website. http://www.thefamily.com/poetry/annaspoems.html

Jurica, Alice B. "Good Friday." *Christ in Poetry*. Association Press: New York, 1952. 113.

Oursler, Fulton. Excerpt. *The Greatest Story Ever Told*. Walker and Company: New York, 1949. 425–426.

Studdert-Kennedy, G. A. "Gambler." *Christ in Poetry*. Association Press: New York, 1952. 120.

Talmage, James E. "Death and Burial." *Jesus the Christ*. Deseret Book Company: Salt Lake City, 1982. 608–609.

Chapter Four

Akhmatova, Anna. "The One People Once Called." *Divine Inspiration: The Life of Jesus in World Poetry.* Oxford University Press: New York, 1998. 446.

Buechner, Frederich. Excerpt. *Telling the Truth: The Gospel as Tragedy, Comedy, and Fairy Tale.* Harper San Francisco, a Division of Harper Collins Publishers: New York, 1977. 11–14.

Calvin, John. "John 19:19–22." *Commentary on the Gospel According to John.* Wm. B. Eerdmans Publishing Company: Grand Rapids, 1949. 227–229.

Card, Michael. Excerpt. *A Violent Grace.* Multnomah Publishers, Inc.: Sisters, OR, 2000. 72.

Dickinson, Emily. "One Crown Not Any Seek." Public Domain.

Flavel, John. "Sermon 27." *Fountain of Life.* Public Domain.

Foxe's Book of Martyrs. Excerpt. Whitaker House: Springdale, 1981. 26–27.

Henry, Matthew. "John 19." *Commentary on the Whole Bible.* Public Domain.

Hopkins, Gerard Manley. "And Joseph and His Mother Marveled." *Tongues of Angels, Tongues of Men.* Doubleday: New York, 1999.

Shillito, Edward. "Ave Crux, Spes Unica!" *Masterpieces of Religious Verse.* Harper & Brothers Publishers: New York, 1948.

Spurgeon, Charles H. "April 7 Morning." *Morning & Evening.* The Old Time Gospel Hour: Lynchburg, VA. Public Domain.

Chapter Five

Borges, Jorge Luis. "Luke XXIII." *The Gospels in Our Image.* Harcourt Brace & Company: New York, 1995. 211.

Burnham, Richard. "Jesus, Thou Art the Sinner's Friend." Public Domain.

Crouse, Miriam LeFevre. "Upon a Hill." *Christ in Poetry.* Association Press: New York, 1952. 119.

Kresensky, Raymond. "The Suffering God," *Christ in Poetry.* Association Press: New York, 1952. 117.

MacLagen, William D. "Lord, When Thy Kingdom Comes." *Hymns Ancient and Modern.* Public Domain.

Mirick, Edith. "Two Others on Either Side." *Christ in Poetry.* Association Press: New York, 1952. 118.

Neuhaus, Richard John. "Judge Not." *Death on a Friday Afternoon.* Basic Books of the Perseus Books Group: New York, 2000.

O'Brien, Isidore. Excerpt. *The Life of Christ.* St. Anthony Guild Press: Paterson, 1937.

Robinson, Edwin Arlington. "Calvary." *The Gospels in Our Image.* Harcourt Brace & Company: New York, 1995. 208.

Thomas, G. Ernest. "Hope for All Humanity." *Daily Meditations on the Seven Last Words.* Abingdon Press: New York, 1959.

Chapter Six

Athanasius of Alexandria. Quote. Public Domain.

Grant, Myrna Reid. "Plain Fact." *A Widening Light: Poems of the Incarnation.* Harold Shaw Publishers: Wheaton, 1997. 109.

Hedrick, Addie M. "Two Crosses." *Christ in Poetry.* Association Press: New York, 1952. 116.

Meynell, Alice. "Easter." *The Lion Christian Poetry Collection.* Lion Publishing Corporation: 1995. 313.

Morgan, George Campbell. "The Darkness of Golgotha." *Classic Sermons on the Cross of Christ,* compiled by Warren W. Wiersbe. Hendrickson Publishers: Grand Rapids: 1990. 145–147.

Noll, Mark A. "Et Resurrexit Tertia Die (Bach, *Credo,* B-minor Mass)." *A Widening Light: Poems of the Incarnation.* Harold Shaw Publishers: Wheaton, 1997. 113.

Oursler, Fulton. Excerpt. *The Greatest Story Ever Told.* Walker and Company: New York, 1949. 426.

Pitman, Marion. "Easter Midnight Service." *The Lion Christian Poetry Collection.* Lion Publishing Corporation: 1995. 311.

Rooney, Elizabeth. "Easter Saturday." *The Lion Christian Poetry Collection.* Lion Publishing Corporation: 1995. 311.

Skeath, William. "The Darkness of Moral Despair." *His Last Words.* Cokesbury Press: Nashville, 1939. 51–52.

Stewart, Desmond. Excerpt. *The Foreigner: A Search for the First-Century Jesus.* Hamish Hamilton: London, 1981. 146.

Thrilling, Isobel. "Before Easter." *The Lion Christian Poetry Collection.* Lion Publishing Corporation: 1995. 309.

Watts, Isaac. "Alas! and Did My Saviour Bleed." Public Domain.

Chapter Seven

Akhmatova, Anna. "Crucifixion." *The Gospels in Our Image.* Harcourt Brace & Company: New York, 1995. 216.

His Last Words. Unknown. Untitled. Cokesbury Press: Nashville, 1939. 50.

Lawrence, D. H. "Eloi, Eloi, Lama Sabachthani?" *The Gospels in Our Image.* Harcourt Brace & Company: New York, 1995. 219–221.

Lewis, C. S. Excerpt. *The Screwtape Letters.* Simon & Schuster: New York, 1961. 41–42.

O'Brien, Isidore. Excerpt. *The Life of Christ.* St. Anthony Guild Press: Paterson, 1937.

Quasimodo, Salvatore. "Anno Domini MCMXLVII." *The Gospels in Our Image.* Harcourt Brace & Company: New York, 1995. 224.

"Savior Speaks, The." Anonymous. *The Lion Christian Poetry Collection.* Lion Publishing Corporation: 1995. 302.

Skeath, William. "The Darkness of Moral Despair." *His Last Words.* Cokesbury Press: Nashville, 1939. 52–60.

Thomas, G. Ernest. "God as Seen in Christ." *Daily Meditations on the Seven Last Words.* Abingdon Press: Nashville, 1954. 78–80.

Walsh, Chad. "Why Hast Thou Forsaken Me?" *A Widening Light: Poems of the Incarnation.* Harold Shaw Publishers: Wheaton, 1984. 100.

Chapter Eight

His Last Words. Unknown. Untitled. Cokesbury Press: Nashville, 1939. 62.

Holme, Vincent. "Good Friday." *Christ in Poetry.* Association Press: New York, 1952. 139.

McElroy, John Alexander. "The Fifth Word." *Living with the Seven Words.* Abingdon Press: New York, 1961. 38–40.

O'Brien, Isidore. Excerpt. *The Life of Christ.* St. Anthony Guild Press: Paterson, 1937. 497–498.

Roberts, Frederick T. "The Cup." *Christ in Poetry.* Association Press: New York, 1952. 139.

Shea, Walter. "Crusts." *Christ in Poetry.* Association Press: New York, 1952. 138.

Skeath, William C. "A Spiritual Thirst." *His Last Words.* Cokesbury Press: Nashville, 1939. 63–68.

Thomas, G. Ernest. "Jesus Speaks for the Needy." *Daily Meditations on the Seven Last Words.* Abingdon Press: New York, 1959. 89–91.

Turnbull, Ralph G. "The Word of Suffering." *The Seven Words from the Cross.* Baker Book House: Grand Rapids, 1959. 36–41.

Chapter Nine

Augustine of Hippo. "What We Behold on the Cross." Public Domain.

Brown, Sir Thomas. Excerpt. Public Domain.

Card, Michael. Excerpt. *Immanuel: Reflections on the Life of Christ.* Thomas Nelson, Inc.: Nashville, 1990.

————. Excerpt. *Immanuel: Reflections on the Life of Christ.* Thomas Nelson, Inc.: Nashville, 1990.

————. "Here I Stand." *Immanuel: Reflections on the Life of Christ.* Thomas Nelson, Inc.: Nashville, 1990. 183–185.

————. "This Must Be the Lamb." *Immanuel: Reflections on the Life of Christ.* Thomas Nelson, Inc.: Nashville, 1990. 177–181.

Donne, John. "Good Friday, 1613. Riding Westward." *The Lion Christian Poetry Collection.* Lion Publishing Corporation: 1995. 306.

Fletcher, Giles. "Palm Sunday: Good Friday." *The Lion Christian Poetry Collection.* Lion Publishing Corporation: 1995. 298.

"Good Friday." Anonymous. *The Lion Christian Poetry Collection.* Lion Publishing Corporation: 1995. 301.

Lewis, C. S. Excerpt. *The Lion, the Witch, and the Wardrobe.* Macmillan Publishing Company: New York, 1977.

Milton, John. "On the Significance of the Son of God." *Paradise Lost.* Public Domain.

Muir, Edwin. "The Killing." *The Gospels in Our Image.* Harcourt Brace & Company: New York, 1995. 222–223.

Peterson, Eugene H. "Reminder." *A Widening Light: Poems of the Incarnation.* Harold Shaw Publishers: Wheaton, 1997. 98.

Victor, Christus. "Pange, lingua." Public Domain.

Watts, Isaac. "When I Survey the Wondrous Cross." Public Domain.

Chapter Ten

Card, Michael. "He Was Heard." *Immanuel: Reflections on the Life of Christ.* Thomas Nelson, Inc.: Nashville, 1990.

Chambers, Oswald. Excerpt. *My Utmost for His Highest.* 105.

Edwards, Jonathan. Quote. *Pardon for the Greatest Sinner.* From the Grace Baptist Church of Canton, Michigan website. http://www.jonathan edwards.com/sermons/Doctrine/pardon.htm

Lewis, C. S. Excerpt. *The Lion, the Witch, and the Wardrobe.* Macmillan Publishing Company: New York, 1995.

Maiuzzo, Naomi. "Remember Me." Sincerely Yours Christian Poetry website. http://www.bsincere.ntinternet.co.uk/christianpoetry15.html

Newton, John. "Approach, My Soul, the Mercy Seat." *Olney Hymns.* Public Domain.

Pounds, Wil. "The Veil in the Temple." Abide in Christ website. http://www.abideinchrist.org/messages/mat2751.html

Sevier, Randal. Excerpt. *The Torn Veil.* Solo Christo website. http://www.solochristo.com/theology/nct/veil.htm

Spurgeon, C. H. "The Rent Veil." The Spurgeon Archive website. http://www.spurgeon.org/sermons/2015.htm

Stowell, Hugh. "From Every Stormy Wind." *The Winter's Wreath, a Collection of Original Contributions in Prose and Verse.* 1828. Public Domain.

Swindoll, Charles. Excerpt. *The Preeminent Person of Christ.* Insight for Living: Plano, 1990. 155.

Wesley, Charles. "'Tis Finished! The Messiah Dies." *Short Hymns.* 1762. Public Domain.

Chapter Eleven

Baker, Henry W. "Lord Jesus God and Man." Public Domain.

Calvin, John. Excerpt. Calvin's Commentaries website. http://www.ccel.org/c/calvin/comment3/comm_index.htm. Public Domain.

Channing, William Ellery. An Example Without Rival. Public Domain.

Cobb, Irvin S. Excerpt. *Behold the Man.* Public Domain.

Dr. Maclear's New Testament History. Untitled. Public Domain.

Eddy, Mary Baker. "On Jesus as the Son of God." Public Domain.

Goodling, David. Excerpt. *According to Luke.* William B. Eerdmans Publishing Company: Grand Rapids, 1987. 345.

Heermann, Johann. "The Centurion's Final Thought." *Ah, Holy Jesus, How Has Thou Offended.* Public Domain.

Hutchcraft, Ron. Excerpt. *A Word with You.* Ron Hutchcraft Ministries, Inc. website. 1996.

Kroll, Woodrow. "The Centurion: Voice of Affirmation." *The Twelve Voices of Easter.* Back to the Bible website. http://www.backtothebible.org/radio/today/17542.

Lucado, Max. Excerpt. *No Wonder They Call Him the Savior.* Multnomah Publishers, Inc.: Sisters, OR. 2001. 77.

———. Excerpt. *No Wonder They Call Him the Savior.* Multnomah Publishers, Inc.: Sisters, 2001.

———. Excerpt. *Six Hours One Friday.* Multnomah Publishers, Inc.: Sisters, OR. 1999. 167–171.

MacArthur, John. Excerpt. *The Murder of Jesus.* Word Publishing, Inc.: Nashville, 2000. 227, 235–238.

McCheyne, Robert Murray. "Christ's Desire for His Saints." Public Domain.

Paassen, Pierre van. "When the Cross Returns." *Behold the Man.* Public Domain. 367.

Pounds, Wil. "The Centurion's Testimony at Jesus' Death." *Father into Thy Hands.* Abide in Christ website. http://www.abideinchrist.com/messages/lk23v46.html.

Rosania, Jenny. "Mighty in Spirit." InTouch Ministries, Atlanta.

Rousseau, Jean Jacques. Quote. Public Domain.

St. Augustine. "Sermon LXXIII." Public Domain.

White, J. Eugene. Excerpt. *The Drama of the Cross.* Baker Book House: Grand Rapids, 1968. 68–69.

Yancey, Philip. Excerpt. *The Jesus I Never Knew.* Zondervan Publishing House: Grand Rapids, 2002. 203.

Chapter Twelve

Bridaine, Jacques. "My Lord, My Master, at Thy Feet Adoring." Public Domain.

Bunyan, John. Excerpt. *The Pilgrim's Progress.* Public Domain.

Donne, John. "The Annunciation and Passion." *Poems of John Donne, Vol. I.* E. K. Chambers, ed. Lawrence & Bullen: London, 1896.

———. "To the Lady Magdalen Herbert, of St. Mary Magdalen." *Poems of John Donne, Vol. I.* E. K. Chambers, ed. Lawrence & Bullen: London, 1896.

Droste-Hulshoff, Annette von. "Gethsemane." *Divine Inspiration: The Life of Jesus in World Poetry.* Oxford University Press: New York, 1998. 403–404.

Elliot, Ebenezer. "The Three Marys at Castle Howard, in 1812 and 1837." *A Sacrifice of Praise.* Cumberland House Publishing: Nashville, 1999.

Fletcher, Giles. "The Celestial City from Christ's Triumph After Death." *A Sacrifice of Praise.* Cumberland House Publishing: Nashville, 1999.

Gore-Booth, Eva. "Crucifixion." *A Sacrifice of Praise.* Cumberland House Publishing: Nashville, 1999.

Hankey, Katherine. "I Love to Tell the Story." *A Sacrifice of Praise.* Cumberland House Publishing: Nashville, 1999.

Henry, Matthew. "Mark 15:40, 41." *Commentary on the Whole Bible.* Public Domain.

"Lament of Our Lady Under the Cross." Anonymous. *Divine Inspiration: The Life of Jesus in World Poetry.* Oxford University Press: New York, 1998.

Lewis, C. S. Excerpt. *The Lion, the Witch, and the Wardrobe.* Macmillan Publishing Company: New York, 1977.

Meynell, Alice. "Easter Night." *A Sacrifice of Praise.* Cumberland House Publishing: Nashville, 1999.

"Near the Cross." Unknown. *Masterpieces of Religious Verse.* Harper & Brothers Publishers: New York, 1948. 186–187.

Newton, John. "The Encounter." *A Sacrifice of Praise.* Cumberland House Publishing: Nashville, 1999.

Shaw, Luci. "Onlookers." *A Sacrifice of Praise.* Cumberland House Publishing: Nashville, 1999.

Todi, Jacapone da. "Stabat Mater." *Divine Inspiration: The Life of Jesus in World Poetry.* Oxford University Press: New York, 1998. 475–476.

Trumbull, Rose. "Mary." *Masterpieces of Religious Verse.* Harper & Brothers Publishers: New York, 1948. 149.

Index of Authors

Index of Titles

We invite you
to complete your Anthology collection . . .

The Incarnation
ISBN: 0-7852-4928-1

The first title in Nelson's Anthology Series depicts the birth of Jesus Christ, as told in both the opening chapters of Matthew and Luke. Stories of celebration and praise for the glorious event of the Incarnation also include 8 beautiful pages of treasured artwork reflecting this momentous event in history.

Also makes a wonderful gift at Christmas time and for new believers any time of year.

Look for future titles at your favorite Christian bookstore.

Also available for your library . . .

Nelson's Personal Handbook on Prayer

Dr. James Wilhoit
ISBN: 0-7852-4880-3

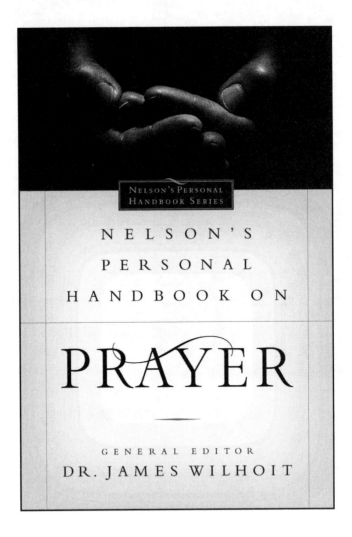

Look for future titles at your favorite Christian bookstore.